TWO-WAY STREET

SECOND EDITION

Communicative English Practice to Build Confidence & Proficiency

by Michael Greisamer

大学教育出版

Table of Contents

Chapter		Function / Usage	Page
1	Is anyone sitting here?	Where are you from? Be questions	2
2	What time does it start?	What time is it? Time	9
3	Today`s my Birthday..	Dates / Talking about dates	13
4	Do you know how to...	Can / Talking about abilities	17
5	You always watch TV!	Daily Routine Frequency adverbs	26
6	Ouch! That hurts.	Body parts / illness Have/had Should/Advice	32
7	Practice makes perfect	Review Chapter 1-6	40
8	Which way is up?	Map / giving directions Could you tell me...?	46
9	Where does this go?	Describing location of objects Preposition of place	54
10	All in the Family	Getting personal Talking about family	59
11	Ready to order?	Ordering in Restaurant Describing food	64
12	Why, thank you!	Giving & Responding to Compliments	70
13	Practice makes Perfect	Review Chapter 8-12	75
14	SKIT	Group speaking Presentation practice	81
	INTERVIEW PROJECT		91

1

Practice the dialog with your partner

(A) : Is anyone sitting here?
(B) : No, go ahead.
(A) : Hi, my name is <u>Lorrie</u>.
(B) : Hello. My name is <u>Shiho</u>.
(A) : Nice to meet you, <u>Shiho</u>. Where are you from?
(B) : I'm from <u>Nagoya</u> and live in <u>New York City</u> now.
(A) : Oh, really. I'm from <u>Los Angeles</u>.
(B) : Oh, yeah? What part?
(A) : I'm from <u>Torrance</u>.
(B) : Oh, we had better* be quiet, the teacher is starting to talk.

*had better = should

Practice more by substituting the <u>underlined parts</u>.

 Speaker 1.   Speaker 2.

1

(A) Name : Ross
From : Canada
Part : Toronto

(B) Name : Amy
From : Chicago
Lives in : Mexico City

2

(A) Name : Scott
From : Australia
Part : Perth

(B) Name : Yoshiko
From : Awaji Island
Lives in : Akashi

Is anyone sitting here?

NAMES

John Fitzgerald Kennedy

First Name   Middle Name   Last Name

Lets work on first names.
Listen & repeat.

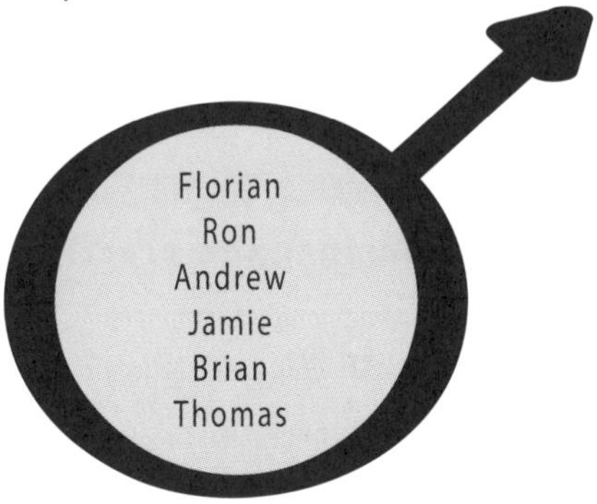

Florian
Ron
Andrew
Jamie
Brian
Thomas

Maria
Bridget
Millie
Beth
Carolyn
Angela

Do you know any other names?
(not Japanese)

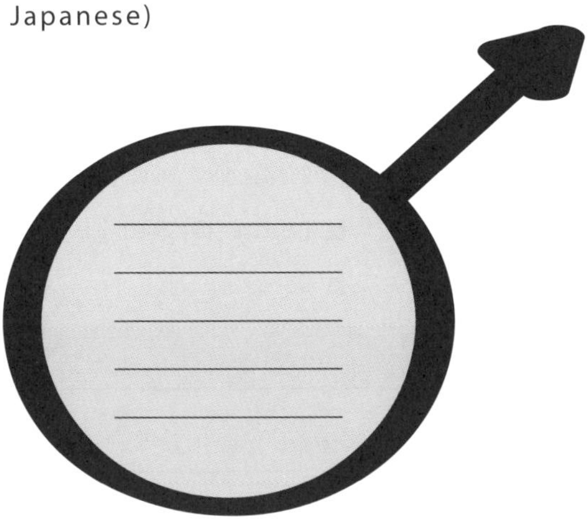

Now add your names to the list on the board.

1st STEP — Matching

What's your name?	☐	☐	Her name is Tina.
What's his name?	☐	☐	Their names are Bob and Susan.
What's her name?	☐	☐	My name is Yoshiko.
What are their names?	☐	☐	His name is Ralph.
Where are you from?	☐	☐	I live in Mexico City.
Where is he from?	☐	☐	They are from Saitama.
Where is she from?	☐	☐	He is from Melbourne.
Where are they from?	☐	☐	She's from Paris.
Where do you live?	☐	☐	I'm from Taidera.
Where does he live?	☐	☐	They live in Los Angeles.
Where do they live?	☐	☐	I don't know where he lives.

Check your answers with your partner and practice.

2nd STEP — More Matching

What are your hobbies?	☐	☐	They are in the tennis club.
What are his hobbies?	☐	☐	I like to play racquetball.
What are her hobbies?	☐	☐	My hobby is dancing.
What are their hobbies?	☐	☐	Her hobbies are skiing and watching movies.
What club are you in?	☐	☐	I am in the computer club.
What club is he in?	☐	☐	She likes ice hockey.
What club is she in?	☐	☐	His hobbies are diving and water-skiing.
What club are they in?	☐	☐	Their hobbies are riding horses and cooking.
What kind of sports do you like?	☐	☐	She's in the drama club.
What kind of sports does he like?	☐	☐	He doesn't like sports.
What kind of sports does she like?	☐	☐	He's not in a club.

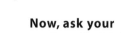

Now, ask your partner for his/her real answers and write his/her answers.

My partner's name is : _____

My partner is from : _____

My partner lives in : _____

— 4 —

3rd STEP
Ask Speaker 2

Is anyone sitting here?

Speaker 1 page

KEY
① = Name(s)?
② = From?
③ = Live?
④ = Hobby?

a

① _____
② Finland
③ _____
④ Fishing

b

① Maria
② Mexico
③ _____
④ _____

c

① Florian
② _____
③ Munich
④ _____

d

① _____
② _____
③ Amsterdam
④ Riding horses

e

① Patty / Johnny
② _____
③ Melbourne
④ _____

f

① Jamie & Kim
② _____
③ Ocean City
④ _____

g

① Rocky
② _____
③ _____
④ Chasing cats

h

① _____
② California
③ _____
④ Traveling

1

3rd STEP
Ask Speaker 1

Speaker 2 page

KEY
① = Name(s)?
② = From?
③ = Live?
④ = Hobby?

a

① Kevin
②
③ London
④

b

①
②
③ New York City
④ Drawing

c

①
② Germany
③
④ Skiing

d
① Angela
② Nebraska
③
④

e

①
② Perth
③
④ People watching

f

①
② Palmyra
③
④ Going to the movies

g

①
② Doggieville
③ Pooch City
④

h

① Ron & Nancy
②
③ Washington D.C.
④

— 6 —

Is anyone sitting here?

Use It
KEY

① = Name(s)?
② = From?
③ = Live?
④ = Hobbies?
⑤ = *Other Info?

Your Information

①
②
③
④
⑤

* Questions for "Other Info."

Tell me something about yourself.

or

What is your other info?

Greetings / Openings
- Hi there / Howdy
- How have ya been?
- Good to see you.
- How are things?
- What's up?

Closings
- Well, talk to you later.
- See you later.
- Take it easy.
- Have a good one.

Usage Hint

Use "**And you?**" & "**How about you?**" when you want to ask the same question to someone else.

— 7 —

1

5th STEP

Stand up. Walk around.
Meet 8 different people.
Write about them.

For Example

Jiro	:	Hello, my name is Jiro. What's your name?
Yukie	:	My name is Yukie. Where are you from, Jiro?
Jiro	:	I'm from Tarumi. How about you?

KEY

① = Name(s)?
② = From?
③ = Live?
④ = Hobbies?
⑤ = *Other Info?

2 What time does it start?

Practice the dialog with your partner

David : Let's go to the movies.
Anna : Okay. What do you wanna* see?
David : How about <u>Star Wars?</u> (a)
Anna : Well, there's a show at <u>6 O'clock and 8:30.</u> (b)
David : Oh, and you know I really wanna see <u>Superman Returns</u>! (c)
Anna : Humm, It starts at <u>5:50 and 9:10</u>. (d)
David : Oh, and what about that new movie that just came out.....
Anna : Hey! Would you make up your mind.

wanna = want to

Philadelphia

Pennsylvania

Practice more by substituting the <u>underlined parts.</u>

Conversation 1	Conversation 2
David (a) **Rocky 10** (c) **Titanic**	(a) **War is Hell** (c) **House of the Vampire**

Anna

(b)

Five fifteen
or
Quarter-past five

Seven thirty
or
Half-past seven

(b)

Eight fifty-five
or
Five before nine

Eleven oh five
or
Five past eleven

(d)

Two twenty-five
or
Twenty-five after two

Three thirty-five
or
Twenty-five to four

(d)

Midnight

– 9 –

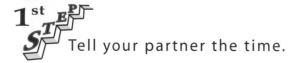

Tell your partner the time.

Speaker 1 page

a b c d

e f g h

Usage Hint

Different Ways to ask the time.
What time is it?
Do you have the time?
Could you please tell me the time?
Do you know what time it is?
Can you tell me the time?

Speaker 1 Ask your partner the time

1 2 3 4

_____ _____ _____ _____

5 6 7 8

_____ _____ _____ _____

What time does it start?

2nd STEP Fill in the blanks by asking your partner.

How to Ask

What's on (DAY) at / from (TIME) on (channel #) ?

What's on (at / from) (TIME) on (channel #) ?

Example :
What's on Friday from 9:30 on Channel 12?

How to Answer

(Program name) (is / are) on (at / from) (TIME) on (channel #)?

Example :
A documentary is on from 9 o'clock on channel 12.
<or>
Star Trek is on at 5 on channel 6.

Speaker 1 page

Speaker 2 go to page # 93

TIME	CHANNEL 3	CHANNEL 6	CHANNEL 10	CHANNEL 12
4:00 p.m.		The Plastic Chef		
4:30 p.m.				
5:00 p.m.	Pokeitmon	Sing for Cash Singing Competition		International News
5:30 p.m.				
6:00 p.m.		Family Guy	Quiz Show	The White House
6:30 p.m.				
7:00 p.m.	School Break *Season 3*			"Que pasa Amigos!" (Learn Spanish)
7:30 p.m.				
8:00 p.m.		Survivor : Living in Japan!		
8:30 p.m.				
9:00 p.m.		"Why Were U Late 4 class?" *(Mystery Movie)*		"How the West Was Won." *(Documentary)*
9:30 p.m.				
10:00 p.m.			Music Station	
10:30 p.m.				
TIME	**CHANNEL 3**	**CHANNEL 6**	**CHANNEL 10**	**CHANNEL 12**
4:00 p.m.			"As the World Churns" *(Soap Opera)*	
4:30 p.m.				
5:00 p.m.	Glee *Season 1*			*(write your answer)**
5:30 p.m.				
6:00 p.m.		The Chimpsons	Professional Baseball Game Tigers vs Hawks	Keepin'-fit Exercise Show
6:30 p.m.				
7:00 p.m.	The M-Files			
7:30 p.m.				
8:00 p.m.	"Star Bars" *(Science Fiction Movie)*			National Geographic
8:30 p.m.				
9:00 p.m.			Late Night With David Bekermen	
9:30 p.m.				
10:00 p.m.				
10:30 p.m.				

FRIDAY

SATURDAY

*Write your favorite TV show.

– 11 –

2. What time does it start?

TV guide Expansion Matching

1	C. S. I.		a	A situation comedy, usually 30 minutes. (Friends, Full House)
2	Soap Opera		b	A spoof of the Italian opera, Madame Butterfly (蝶々夫人).
3	Glee		c	An afternoon drama
4	G-Force		d	A popular afternoon talk show staring Oprah Winfrey.
5	Peanuts		e	A cartoon with the snoopy characters.
6	Madame Butterfingers		f	A spoof of the science fiction drama X-files.
7	The Oprah Winfrey show		g	A reality show in which contestant must survive a difficult situation, like living in the jungle or on an island.
8	Survivor		h	A spoof of the sitcom, The Simpson.
9	Chimpsons		i	Crime Scene Investigation
10	M-files		j	An old Japanese animation, called "Gachaman" in Japanese.
11	Sit-com		k	A musical comedy-drama TV series that focuses on a high school glee club.

The **More or Less** game (7 guesses)

How to play

Pick an object and have your partner guess the price.
For example: your pen, watch or jacket.
Say "more" or "less" until your partner guesses the answer.

For Example

Speaker 1 : How much are these shoes?
　　　　　　　(pointing at your shoes)
Speaker 2 : Your shoes cost 3,000 yen.
Speaker 1 : No, less!
Speaker 2 : I think they cost 2,000 yen.
Speaker 1 : More!
Speaker 2 : 2,500 yen.
Speaker 1 : Yes, that's right.

$ $ $ $ $

Need to Know.

100	= One hundred
200	= Two hundred
300	= Three hundred
1,000	= One thousand
2,000	= Two thousand
3,000	= Three thousand
10,000	= Ten thousand
20,000	= Twenty thousand

Usage Hint

Different Ways to ask the price:
What is the price of this?
How much is this?
How much do you think this costs?

3 Today's my birthday!

Practice the dialog with your partner

Nick : Hi. How have you been?

Joanne : Not bad thanks. How about you?

Nick : Pretty good. Do you have the time?

Joanne : Yeah. It's 3:30 (three thirty).

Nick : Thanks.

Joanne : Do you know today's date?

Nick : Uhh, yeah, its <u>April 1st (first)</u>.

Joanne : Oh, wow. Today is <u>April Fool's day</u>.

Nick : That's right.

Practice more, with <u>other dates</u>.

January
15th
*Coming of
Age Day*

February
14th
*Valentine's
Day*

March
17th
*St. Patrick's
Day*

April
1st
*April Fool's
Day*

May
3rd
*Constitution
Day*

June
14th
*Flag
Day*

July
7th
*Star
Festival*

August
17th
*Our Teacher's
Birthday*

September
23rd
*The First Day
of Autumn*

October
31st
Halloween

November
3rd
*Culture
Day*

December
31st
*New Year's
Eve*

3

Need to Know.

Days of the Week

Monday   (M)
Tuesday   (Tu)
Wednesday   (W)
Thursday   (Th)
Friday   (F)
Saturday   (Sa)
Sunday   (Su)

MONTHS

English | french | german | japanese

January | janvier | Januar | 一月
February | février | Februar | 二月
March | mars | März | 三月
April | avril | April | 四月
May | mai | Mai | 五月
June | juin | Juni | 六月
July | juillet | Juli | 七月
August | août | August | 八月
September | septembre | September | 九月
October | octobre | Oktober | 十月
November | novembre | November | 十一月
December | décembre | Dezember | 十二月

DATES

1st	=	First	16th	=	Sixteenth
2nd	=	Second	17th	=	Seventeenth
3rd	=	Third	18th	=	Eighteenth
4th	=	Fourth	19th	=	Nineteenth
5th	=	Fifth	20th	=	Twentieth
6th	=	Sixth	21st	=	Twenty-first
7th	=	Seventh	22nd	=	Twenty-second
8th	=	Eighth	23rd	=	Twenty-third
9th	=	Ninth	24th	=	Twenty-fourth
10th	=	Tenth	25th	=	Twenty-fifth
11th	=	Eleventh	26th	=	Twenty-sixth
12th	=	Twelfth	27th	=	Twenty-seventh
13th	=	Thirteenth	28th	=	Twenty-eighth
14th	=	Fourteenth	29th	=	Twenty-ninth
15th	=	Fifteenth	30th	=	Thirtieth
			31th	=	Thirty-first

YEARS

1885 = Eighteen eighty-five
1969 = Nineteen sixty-nine
1982 = Nineteen eighty-two
2011 = Twenty eleven
2016 = Twenty sixteen

Usage Hint

Pronunciation of 30, 40, 50, 60, 70, and 80. Sometimes the "t" is pronounce with a "d".
Example :
    thir"d"y
    thir"d"ieth
    fif"d"y
    fif"d"ieth

Today's my birthday!

1st STEP — PAST EVENTS & DATES
Ask Speaker 2, & write the answers.

Speaker 1 page
Speaker 2 go to page # 96

S1 : When was _____ ? *(event)*
S2 : It was _____. *(date)*

S1 : Tell me what happened on _____. *(date)*
(or) Do you know what happened on _____? *(date)*
S2 : _____ *(event)*

EVENT	DATE
The end of World War Two for Japan....................	
The World Trade Center bombing.............................	
Miyazaki awarded Picture of the Year for Princess Mononoke	
The Atomic bomb dropped on Hiroshima................	
The Showa era changed to The Heisei era...............	
	7/4/1776
	5/15/1972
	6/1/1949
	4/28/1952
	7/20/1969

Tell Speaker 2 the answers.

Answer

The Great Hanshin Earthquake	1/17/1995
The first Japanese woman in space (C. Mukai)	7/8/1994
President F.D. Roosevelt "Four Freedoms" speech	1/6/1941
The Japanese attack on Pearl Harbor	12/7/1941
Adolf Hitler named Chancellor of Germany	1/31/1933
The capital was relocated from Kyoto to Tokyo	3/28/1869
Princess Diana fatal car accident	8/31/1997
President Kennedy was shot	11/16/1963
The Hanshin Tigers won the championship	9/15/2003
The North / South Korean Summit	6/18/2000

How to play

1. Draw 7 ships anywhere on your battle grid.

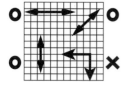

Hit or Miss

DATES

Your Sea-Battle Grid	1	2	3	4	5	6	11	13	21	27	30	31
January												
February												
March												
April												
May												
June												
July												
August												
September												
October												
November												
December												

Your Fleet

Submarine

Draw 2 submarines
(2 squares each)

Destroyer

Draw 3 destroyers
(3 squares each)

Battleship

Draw 2 battleships
(4 squares each)

2. Take turns saying different dates.
   Mark your partner's shots in the small battle grid.

"June Third!" "HIT!" "MISS!" "Hit and Sunk!" "You sank my Battleship!"

Speaker 1 : August first
Speaker 2 : That's a Miss!
              May twenty-seventh.
Speaker 1 : That's a hit!

Your mission is to destroy all the enemy ships.

Your partner's Sea-Battle Grid	1	2	3	4	5	6	11	13	21	27	30	31
January												
February												
March												
April												
May												
June												
July												
August												
September												
October												
November												
December												

* *On a calender February has 28 days, April, June, September and November only have 30 days.*

4 Do you know how to...?

Practice the dialog with your partner

Louise : By the way, what do you do?
George : Pardon me?
Louise : I said, what do you do?
George : I'm sorry, I don't understand.
Louise : Oh... What is your job?
George : Oh, I'm studying to be <u>a chef</u>.
Louise : How interesting!
      Can you <u>bake a cake</u>?
George : No not yet, I'm still learning.

Grammar Hint
"Pretty good" used after the "be" verb is okay.
After any other verb, it should be "pretty well"
example :
I can cook pretty well.
I'm pretty good.
or
I'm okay.

Practice more by substituting the <u>underlined parts</u>.

a pilot	an architect	a musician	an artist
fly a jet?	design a house?	play the guitar?	paint a picture?

4

1st STEP

Check the correct box. ✓

Grammar Hint

Do not use "pretty well" with be verb.
Use "pretty good" after be verb.
After other verbs, both are fine.
example :
I can cook pretty well.
I can cook pretty good.
I'm pretty good.

1 Can he ride a bicycle?
- ☐ a. Yes, she can.
- ☐ b. Yes, he can.

2 Does she know how to play tennis?
- ☐ a. No she doesn't.
- ☐ b. No, they don't.

3 Do you know how to make spaghetti sauce?
- ☐ a. Yeah, I'm pretty well.
- ☐ b. Yeah, pretty well.

4 Do you know how to play soccer?
- ☐ a. No, I'm not very well.
- ☐ b. Not very well.

5 Can you use a computer?
- ☐ a. No, I'm very good.
- ☐ b. Nah, not at all.

6 Can you speak English?
- ☐ a. Yes, you can.
- ☐ b. Yes, but only a little.

7 Can they play badminton?
- ☐ a. No, not very well.
- ☐ b. No, she can't.

8 Can they drive a truck?
- ☐ a. Yeah, I can.
- ☐ b. Yeah, I think so.

9 Can you eat natto?
- ☐ a. No, I hate it.
- ☐ b. No, it hates me.

10 Could you tell me how to get to the station?
- ☐ a. Sure, let me think...
- ☐ b. Sure, I don't know.

Do you know how to...?

3rd STEP

"Yeah, I can." "So can I!"

Think of the question / Write the answers.

SPEAKER 1

SPEAKER 2

1		2		3
Can you.....? or Do you know how to......?	+	YES...	*yes* **Same**	Me too or So can I
		NO...	*no*	Me neither or Neither can I
		NO...	*(yes)* **Different**	Oh really, I can.
		YES...	*(no)*	Oh really, I can't.

Ask your partner and write the answers.

fly a plane
cook Italian food
cook for many people
play golf   speak another language
stay up all night play pool
sky dive   play a musical instrument
play ice hockey   play poker / play cards
drink whiskey   jet ski
type quickly   do math

WE CAN	WE CAN'T

YOU ONLY	PARTNER ONLY

Example dialog :

Speaker 1 : Do you know how to fish?

Speaker 2 : No, I don't.

Speaker 1 : Me neither.

Speaker 2 : Can you play cards?

Speaker 1 : Yes, I can.

Speaker 2 : Oh really, me too.

4

2nd STEP Practice
Pair work with Speaker 2
Circle the correct answer

Chris

Janan

Andrew

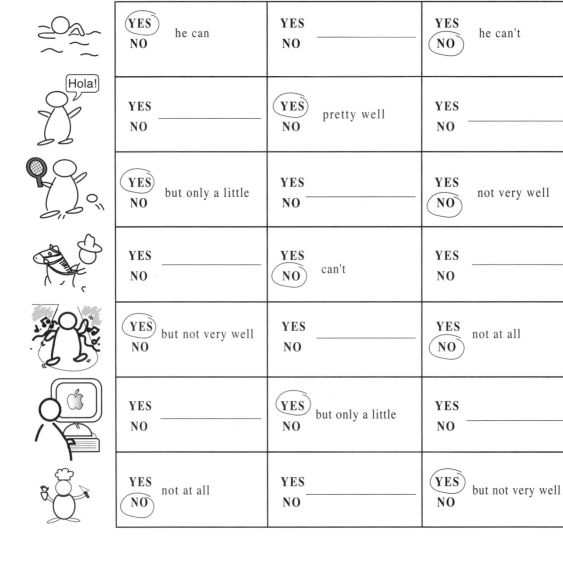

Do you know how to...?

S1 : Can Chris speak Spanish?
S2 : Nah, not at all. Can he swim?
S1 : Yes, he can.

<OR>

S2 : Can Emily dance?
S1 : Yeah, (she can) pretty well. Can she ride a horse?
S2 : Nah, not at all.

	Emily	Rosebud	Jamie & Kim
	YES _____ NO _____	(YES) very well NO	YES _____ NO _____
	(YES) can NO	YES _____ NO _____	(YES) very well NO
	YES _____ NO _____	YES only one time (NO)	YES _____ NO _____
	YES not at all (NO)	YES _____ NO _____	YES can't (NO)
	YES _____ NO _____	(YES) pretty well NO	YES _____ NO _____
	(YES) pretty well NO	YES _____ NO _____	(YES) but only a mac NO
	(YES) she's ok NO	YES _____ NO _____	YES not at all (NO)

- 21 -

4

4th STEP — How to play

Your teacher will give you a number between 1 and 8.
Walk around and ask other people if they can do the things in the box.
Only write the names of those who "can" do it.
Find a different person for each thing.
"?" Write another question to ask.
Try to answer with more than "Yes" or "No".

---

1   Find someone who can :

Play badminton   _____

Ride a scooter   _____

Say, "Hello" in
Spanish   _____

Make pizza   _____

Play the piano   _____

? _____   _____

---

2   Find someone who can :

Ice skate   _____

Play a musical instrument _____

Eat liver   _____

Cook Italian food   _____

Stand on
your head   _____

? _____   _____

---

3   Find someone who can :

Swim very well   _____

Ride a bicycle   _____

Say goodbye in Korean   _____

Drink alcohol   _____

Sing Kimigayo   _____

? _____   _____

---

4   Find someone who can :

Ride a horse   _____

Sing a song
in English   _____

Eat natto   _____

Play tennis   _____

Tie a necktie   _____

? _____   _____

— 22 —

Do you know how to...?

Speaker 1 : Excuse me, do you know how to play badminton?
Speaker 2 : No, I don't, I've never tried. Can you ice skate?
Speaker 1 : Yes, I can, but I have only done it once.
Speaker 2 : Okay, what's your name?

5 Find someone who can :

Eat spicy food _____

Drive a car _____

Snowboard _____

Knit _____

Laugh like a pig _____

? _____

6 Find someone who can :

Sleep anywhere _____

Do Aikido _____

Run fast _____

Sing a song by "AKB48" _____

Surf the internet _____

? _____

7 Find someone who can :

Ride a motorcycle _____

Dance Bon-Odori _____

Use a computer _____

Scuba Dive _____

Play chess _____

? _____

8 Find someone who can :

Throw a Frisbee _____

Twirl a pen _____

Play billiards _____

Laugh like a horse _____

Put on a Kimono _____

? _____

Occupational Crossword Puzzle

Need to Know.

dentist	sales clerk	police
farmer	barber	chef
housewife	teacher	mechanic
director	singer	soldier
fire fighter	waitress	athlete
nurse	postal worker	carpenter
taxi driver	construction worker	

Do you know how to...?

1. I can't repair a car because I'm not a _____ .
6. A _____ _____ (two words) delivers mail to everyone.
9. A _____ works in a restaurant and can take your order.
12. A person who can make movies is called a _____ .
13. Someone who puts out fires and drives a red truck is a _____ (two words).
15. A person who works in a hospital and takes care of sick people is called a _____ .
18. The _____ can protect people and stop crime.
19. A _____ works in a restaurant and can cook very well.
20. Speaker 1 : Can you build a house or a skyscraper?
    Speaker 2 : Yes I can, I'm a _____ (two words).

Grammar Hint
a/an articles
Use before a noun starting with
a consonant : "A" postal worker.
Use "an" before a noun with
a vowel sound : "AN" athlete.

Down

2. Speaker 1 : Do you know how to make things from wood?
   Speaker 2 : Yes I do, I'm a _____ .
3. A person who takes care of the whole house is a _____ .
4. Someone who drives people around in his car all day is a _____ (two words) .
5. Don't let him touch your hair, he is not a _____ .
7. Someone who can teach is a _____ .
8. A _____ _____ (two words) works in a store and helps customers.
10. A person who has a good voice and can sing is a _____.
11. Speaker 1 : Do you know how to clean someone's teeth?
    Speaker 2 : Yes I do, I'm a _____ .
14. A person who grows vegetables and has many animals is called a _____ .
16. I do not have a gun and can't fight, so I would not be a good _____ .
17. An _____ can play sports well.

- 25 -

Practice the dialog with your partner

Angela	:	Hey, let's go out tonight.
Kevin	:	Nah, I wanna* <u>watch TV.</u> (A)
Angela	:	You always <u>watch TV.</u> (A)
Kevin	:	That's not true, sometimes I read a book.
Angela	:	Yeah, but we never go out. You never take me out!
Kevin	:	Okay, let's go to the <u>supermarket.</u> (B)
Angela	:	The <u>supermarket?</u> (B) That's not what I mean.

*wanna = want to

Practice more by substituting the <u>underlined parts</u>.

A: Listen to music / Play video games / Take a nap / Surf the net

B: Drug store / Liquor store / Convenience store / Hardware store

You always watch TV!

Frequency Adverbs

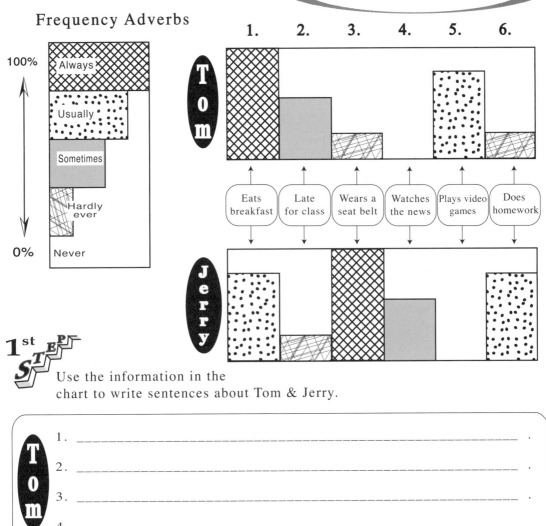

1st STEP

Use the information in the chart to write sentences about Tom & Jerry.

Tom
1. _____.
2. _____.
3. _____.
4. _____.
5. _____.
6. _____.

Jerry
1. _____.
2. _____.
3. _____.
4. _____.
5. _____.
6. _____.

5

2nd STEP

Partner Interview ① Write your daily activities, then tell your partner.

For Example

eat breakfast
read the newspaper
study
clean your room
cook
take a nap
take a bath
go to school
go to work
go out with friends
walk home

TIME		TIME	
_____	Wake Up	_____	
_____		_____	
_____		_____	
_____		_____	
_____		_____	
_____		_____	
_____		_____	
_____		_____	
_____		_____	
_____		_____	
_____		_____	
_____		_____	Go to bed

Example Questions

Do you usually eat breakfast?
What do you do before/after that?
What time do you __ ? (Activity)
What do you do after that?
When do you go to your part time job?
What else?

Grammar Hint Adverbs of Frequency

Usually put the adverb before the verb.
I always check my ....
I hardly ever drink whiskey.
But put the adverb after am.
I "am" sometimes late for class.

② Listen and write your partner's daily activities.

TIME		TIME	
_____	Wakes Up	_____	
_____		_____	
_____		_____	
_____		_____	
_____		_____	
_____		_____	
_____		_____	
_____		_____	
_____		_____	
_____		_____	
_____		_____	
_____		_____	Goes to bed

You always watch TV!

3rd STEP "How Often" Puzzle

① Ask how often your partner does these different things.

Helpful Hints

Listen to Classical music
Play pachinko
Play cards
Go dancing
Go rollerblading
Go to the library
Go to the Opera
Go surfing
Cook
Wash clothes
Clean (your) room
Wear a seat belt
Visit (your) grandparents
Eat out
Over sleep
Read fashion magazines
Think of More!
Anything is okay!

Always

Usually

Sometimes

Hardly ever

Never

Go shopping | go out for dinner
Meet girlfriend or boyfriend | practice archery

For Example

S1 : How often do you surf the internet.
S2 : Well, I hardly ever surf the internet, but I usually play video games on the computer. How about you? Do you ever play video games?
S1 : No, I never play video games. I like to watch TV, I always watch TV in the evening.

go driving | work in the yard or garden
Read a novel | Play baseball

5

4th STEP Use it

IN A ROW 4

Winner

example game grid

Listen to the directions and fill in the blanks.

Okay everyone now we are going to (1) _____ a game. This game is called "Four in a (2) _____. This is a two (3) _____ game, so find a (4) _____. It's better to find a partner that you (5) _____ know very well. Then choose your mark "X" or "O". Use the questions on page number (6) _____. Say a sentence about your partner. If the (7) _____ is correct, place your mark anywhere on the game grid, (round 1). If the answer is (8) _____, the other person can place their mark on the grid. (9) _____ players should use the same book, you don't need to use two books. And both players should say the (10) _____ sentence before going to the next. Ask all questions in order, that means start with #1 and do #2 next, do not (11) _____ questions. For (12) _____ look at the first one; (I think) you usually wake up BEFORE or AFTER 8 am. You must choose (13) _____ or (14) _____ . Then the other person will say "That's right!" or "That's wrong!" To win a round (15) _____ four in a row. Good Luck.

4 IN A ROW SCORE CARD

SPEAKER 1 = X | SPEAKER 2 = O

I think you usually wake up after 8 am.

That's right! I usually wake up after 8.

< or >

That's wrong! I usually wake up BEFORE 8.

ROUND 1 | ROUND 2 | ROUND 3 | ROUND 4 | ROUND 5

ROUND 6 | ROUND 7 | ROUND 8 | ROUND 9 | ROUND 10

Frequency Adverbs

You always watch TV!

For Example

Speaker 1 : I think you usually go to bed after midnight.

Speaker 2 : That's wrong! I usually go to bed before midnight.

(Speaker 2 can put one mark on the game grid)

4 IN A ROW Question List

I think you.....

1. usually wake up *before / after* 8am.
2. usually *eat / don't eat* breakfast.
3. usually eat breakfast *alone / with someone.*
4. *always / never* read the newspaper in the morning.
5. *always / never* watch TV in the morning.
6. usually drink *tea / coffee* in the morning.
7. usually get dressed *before / after* breakfast.
8. usually leave home *before / after* 8:30 am.
9. usually *walk / take the bus* to the station.
10. *usually / hardly ever* exercise.
11. usually eat lunch *before / after* 12:15.
12. usually eat lunch *alone/with someone.*
13. usually *take a nap / don't take a nap* in the afternoon.
14. usually *study / don't study* in the afternoon.
15. usually get home *before / after* 5 o'clock.
16. usually *study / don't study* in the evening.
17. usually take a bath in the *morning / evening.*
18. usually *watch TV / don't watch TV* while eating dinner.
19. usually go to bed *before / after* midnight.
20. usually use a *bed / futon.*
21. *always / never* do your homework.
22. *sometimes / hardly ever* cook dinner.

23. usually eat *rice / bread* for dinner.
24. usually eat dinner *alone /with someone.*
25. *usually/hardly ever* play video games.
26. *usually / hardly ever* come to class.
27. *always / hardly ever* wake up early on Sundays.
28. usually *bring / buy* your lunch.
29. usually take a *bath / shower.*
30. usually talk more to your *mother / father.*
31. *usually / hardly ever* eat sweets.
32. *usually / hardly ever* drink alcohol.
33. *sometimes / hardly ever* go to karaoke.
34. *usually / hardly ever* use a computer.
35. *hardly ever / never* go dancing.
36. *sometimes / hardly ever* go snowboarding.
37. usually go shopping *alone / with someone.*
38. *always / sometimes* go to the convenience store.
39. *usually / hardly ever* read books.
40. **always / never** daydream.
41. **always / sometime** listen to J pop.
42. **usually / never** listen to classical.
43. **usually / hardly ever** listen to reggae

Finished?   THINK OF MORE!

6

Practice the dialog with your partner

Doctor : How are you doing?
Corie : Not so good.
Doctor : What's wrong?
Corie : My <u>leg hurts</u>.
Doctor : That's too bad, what happened?
Corie : I <u>fell off my bicycle</u>.
Doctor : You should be more careful.
Corie : Yeah, you're right.

Grammar Hint
Plural noun + hurt :
  My leg hurt.
Singular noun + hurt :
  My leg hurts.

Practice more by substituting the <u>underlined parts</u>.

head hurts

stomach hurts

feet hurt

eyes hurt

hit the door

ate something strange

ran to school

was surfing the internet all night.

Ouch! That hurts!

1st STEP Mixed Advice

Arrange the word groups to make a sentence

1 you should brush / you should not / your teeth more often / eat sweets and

_____

2 drink so much / boss for a / you shouldn't / day off / and ask your

_____

3 take a hot bath / lift heavy things / you should / and you should not

_____

4 stay up too late / you should / tea and relax / drink some / and you shouldn't

_____

5 you shouldn't / should take vitamins / sleep with / and you / the air conditioner on

_____

6 gets worse / before it / the doctor's office / go to / you should

_____

7 wash / on it / the cut / you should / and / put a band-aid

_____

8 eat such spicy food / you should / and / some stomach medicine / take / you shouldn't

_____

– 33 –

6 2nd STEP — Body Parts

Ask your partner the names of the missing body parts.

Speaker 1 page

Speaker 1 : Is number 3, "mouth"?
Speaker 2 : Yes it is.
Speaker 1 : What is number 9?
Speaker 2 : Number 9, is "chest".
Speaker 1 : How do you spell, "chest"?
Speaker 2 : C-H-E-S-T.

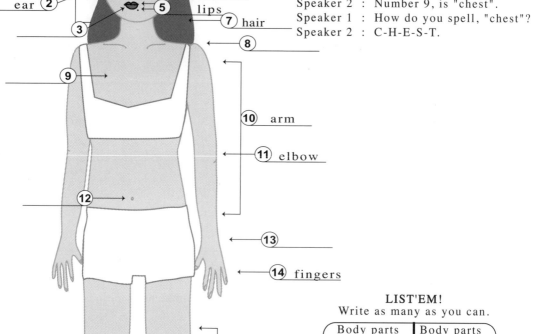

1
ear 2
3
4 eye
6 nose
5 lips
7 hair
8
9
10 arm
11 elbow
12
13
14 fingers
15
16
foot 17
18

LIST'EM!
Write as many as you can.

Body parts you have more than one of.	Body parts you have only one of.
tooth / teeth	mouth

*another word for navel is belly-button.

- 34 -

Ouch! That hurts!

4th STEP — Go to the doctors office

Make a dialog of what you might say when visiting the doctors office.

_____   : _____
_____   : _____
_____   : _____
_____   : _____
_____   : _____
_____   : _____
_____   : _____
_____   : _____
_____   : _____
_____   : _____
_____   : _____

With your partner practice both dialogs.
Choose one and present it to the class.

- 35 -

6 2nd STEP

Body Parts

Ask your partner the names of the missing body parts.

Speaker 2 page

Speaker 1 : Is number 3, "mouth"?
Speaker 2 : Yes it is.
Speaker 1 : What is number 9?
Speaker 2 : Number 9, is "chest".
Speaker 1 : How do you spell, "chest"?
Speaker 2 : C-H-E-S-T.

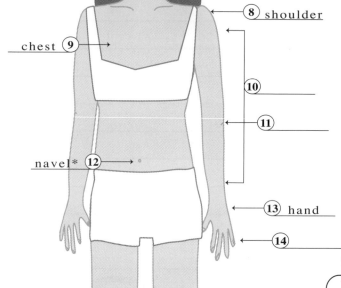

head ①
②
mouth ③
④
⑥
⑤
⑦
⑧ shoulder
chest ⑨
⑩
⑪
navel* ⑫
⑬ hand
⑭
⑮ leg
knee ⑯
⑰
⑱ toes

LIST'EM!
Think of as many as you can.

Body parts you have more than one of.	Singular body parts
tooth / teeth	mouth

*another word for navel is belly-button.

HANGMAN!

Ouch! That hurts!

How to play

1. Work with a partner.
2. One person chooses a word and draws a line for each letter.
   example ___ ___ ___ ___ *(4 letters)*
3. The other person must guess the word before being hung.
4. If a correct letter is said, write the letter above the correct line.
5. If a wrong letter is said draw one body part and write the letter next to the stairs.

For Example

Speaker 1 : Okay, guess the word!
Speaker 2 : Is there a "W"?
Speaker 1 : No, there isn't a "W".
Speaker 2 : Is there an "O"?
Speaker 1 : Yes, there is an "O".
Speaker 2 : "T".
Speaker 1 : No "T".
Speaker 2 : How about an "N"?
Speaker 1 : Did you say, "M"?
Speaker 2 : No, I said, "N".
Speaker 1 : Yeah, there is an "N".

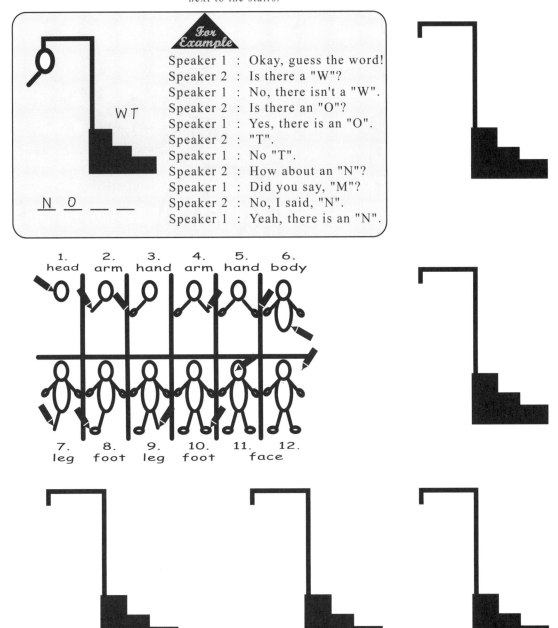

1. head 2. arm 3. hand 4. arm 5. hand 6. body
7. leg 8. foot 9. leg 10. foot 11. 12. face

6

3th STEP

Ask Speaker 2

- Age & Occupation — How old is he/she? What does he/she do?
- What's Wrong? — What's wrong?
- What to do? — What should he/she do?
- What not to do? — What shouldn't he/she do?

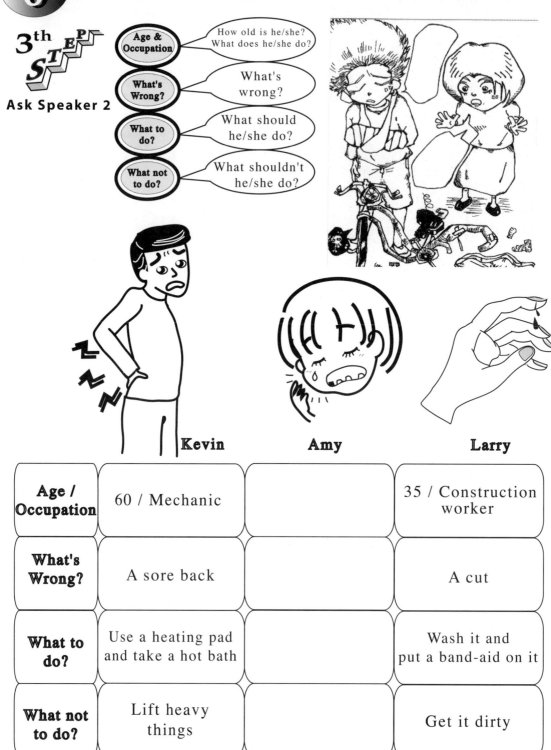

	Kevin	Amy	Larry
Age / Occupation	60 / Mechanic		35 / Construction worker
What's Wrong?	A sore back		A cut
What to do?	Use a heating pad and take a hot bath		Wash it and put a band-aid on it
What not to do?	Lift heavy things		Get it dirty

Ouch! That hurts!

Speaker 1 page — Speaker 2 go to page # 98-99

For Example

Speaker 1 : How old's Pete?
Speaker 2 : He's <u>17</u> years old.
Speaker 1 : What does he do?
Speaker 2 : He is <u>a mechanic</u>.
Speaker 1 : What's wrong?
Speaker 2 : He's <u>got a headache</u>.
Speaker 1 : What should he do?
Speaker 2 : He should <u>take two aspirin and get a massage</u>.
Speaker 1 : What shouldn't he do?
Speaker 2 : He <u>shouldn't listen to loud music or play video games</u>.

Usage Hint

△ = She / her
▯ = He / his 

Evan    Jiro    Angela

	52 / Stock Broker	
	a stomach ache	
	Drink some milk and relax	
	Eat spicy foods	

GAME TIME

How to play

1. Make small groups of 3-5 students.
2. Each person needs a game piece *(ex. eraser or pen cap)*
3. Study the "**GAME KEY**".
4. Use your pencil, close your eyes and touch the "TURN MAKER" numbers.
5. Begin at 'Start Here!', try to go to the Winner's Circle.
6. If a player can't answer the question, the player must go back to his last spot.
   If the player can answer, then he may stay at that spot, and it's the next players' turn.

Game Hints
If nobody knows the answer, ask your friendly teacher.

GAME KEY

All questions must be answered in one minute.

Player must stand up for 30 seconds and do the next thing on the list.

Must correct a sentence from the Correct IT Sentence List. Another player will read a sentence and you must say the correct answer. The correct answers are on page 96.

Make a sentence using the time.

Quick Questions
When a player lands on the "QQ" mark, another player reads a question. The player has ONE MINUTE to answer the question. If the question is not answered in one minute, the player must go back to his last spot.

Practice makes Perfect

When finished check the box ☑ and go to the next one.

'Correct It' Sentence List

- 1. It's a past quarter eleven.
- 2. I can do baseball well.
- 3. Let's go to downtown.
- 4. The pen is on my pocket.
- 5. The table is on the glass.
- 6. It's twelve half.
- 7. What hobby are you?
- 8. What name is you?
- 9. Are you how old?
- 10. Can you do ski?
- 11. Did you go school today?
- 12. How are your hobbies?
- 13. I have a apple.
- 14. I'm Japan.
- 15. Yes, I can't.
- 16. Are you today's date?
- 17. Today is February two.
- 18. Nice to eat you.
- 19. Can you talk English?
- 20. I was born from Osaka.
- 21. Do you play Aikido?
- 22. Do you married?
- 23. Can she swimming?
- 24. Yesterday I saw TV.
- 25. My birthday is October thirty-one.
- 26. Excuse me, do you have the clock?
- 27. It's a doctor's job to stop crime.
- 28. A dentist works at a restaurant.
- 29. A teacher can repair cars.
- 30. Never I wake up early always.
- 31. He ever hardly misses class.
- 32. Excuse me, are you the toilet?
- 33. Excuse me, where is the time?
- 34. Do what do you? (job)
- 35. I usually watch breakfast in the morning.
- 36. Us live in a high-rise apartment building.

Stand up for 30 seconds and act.

Game Hints
Check the back of the book for the correct answers. Page# 97

- Jump up and down.
- Sing a love song.
- Sing your favorite song.
- Sing an English song.
- Pretend you're Ultraman.
- Spin.
- Pretend you're Spiderman.
- Pretend you're a monkey.
- Pretend you're drunk.
- Pretend you're a movie star.
- Pretend you're a chicken.
- Pretend you're a horse.
- Pretend you're a baby.
- Shake your teacher's hand.
- Pretend you're the Prime Minister.
- Draw a face on your hand.
- Pretend you are the teacher.
- Pretend you're the opposite sex.

Quick Questions

- When is your birthday?
- What is today's date?
- How much did your shoes cost?
- What is your cellular phone number?
- Spell your teacher's last name.
- What time do you usually have dinner?
- What time did you go to bed last night?
- What time does this class start?
- What did you do last night? (2 things)
- What did you do yesterday? (2 things)
- What did you do last Sat.? (2 things)
- What are 5 parts of your head?
- What are 5 parts of your body? (not head)
- When is your Father's Birthday?
- What year were you born?
- What is your home phone number?
- Who can build a house or building?
- Who cleans your teeth?
- Count from 11 to 30.
- Count from 20 to 0, backwards.
- Name jobs that start with "C" & "P".
- What is Class Rule Number 1?
- What time is it now?
- Name jobs that start with "A" & "B".
- What is the day before Friday?
- What is the day after Tuesday?
- What is tomorrow's date?
- How do you say "knee" in Japanese?
- How do you say "dentist" in Japanese?
- How do you say "nap" in Japanese?

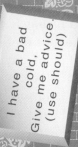

Game Key

 = Correct the sentence

 = Answer the question

 = Make a sentence using the clock

 = Ask & answer the Quick Question

 = Stand up for 30 seconds and do what you are told

SPEED! *How to play*

1. Make small groups of 3-5 people and choose someone to start.
2. The starting person secretly chooses a picture and says a word.
3. The other players try to find the picture.
4. The person who finds the picture, goes next.
5. You get 1 point for each picture you find. The first person to 20, wins!

Next, play by making full sentences. You have to have speed to win!

Memory game

How to play

1. The first person says something about one of the pictures.
2. The next person guesses the picture and adds something using another picture.
3. Go until someone makes a mistake.

Next, try again with full sentences.

S1 : It's 10:15.
S2 : It's 10:15, he's bowling.
S3 : It's 10:15, he's bowling, they're camping.

Practice makes Perfect

STORYBOOK GAME

How to play

Take turns, work together, use the pictures to make a continuing story, each person using one picture.

Game Hint
Use connecting words : "And then", "then", "after that", or "next".

For Example

S1 : Yesterday I was at home listening to music, when I heard a sound.
S2 : The sound was the doorbell, my friend came to visit me.
S3 : We watched TV until 12 o'clock.
S4 : Then we made lunch.
S1 : After that, we cleaned up the dishes and played tennis.

8

Practice the dialog with your partner

Speaker 1 : Excuse me, which way is the <u>Post Office</u>?

Speaker 2 : The <u>Post Office</u>? Uh, turn right at the corner and go straight for two blocks. It's on the right, <u>across from</u> the supermarket.

Speaker 1 : Okay, so I turn right, go two blocks and it's on the right, <u>across from</u> the supermarket?*

Speaker 2 : That's right, you can't miss it.

Speaker 1 : Okay, thanks a lot.

Speaker 2 : You're welcome.

*Claifacation is important

Practice more by substituting the <u>underlined parts</u>.

Police Station	Bank	Hospital	Bus Stop
Behind	Next to	Just past	In front of

Which way is up?

1st STEP

Matching Where is the....?

School? ① ☐	☐ It's near "1".
Hospital? ⑨ ☐	☐ Turn left, it's across from the park just past "6".
Post Office? ⑧ ☐	☐ Its straight ahead.
Internet Cafe? ② ☐	☐ Turn right, it's just past "2", near "9".
Butcher Shop? ③ ☐	☐ It's on the right just before "9".
DVD Rental Shop? ⑥ ☐	☐ It's on the left just past "6" on the corner.
Police Box? ⑤ ☐	☐ It's on the right across from the park.
Bank? ⑦ ☐	☐ It's on the corner, just before "4".
Library? ⑪ ☐	☐ It's on the right between "2" and "3".
Pizza Parlor? ④ ☐	☐ It's on the left across from "2".
Supermarket? ⑩ ☐	☐ It's on the right across from "1".

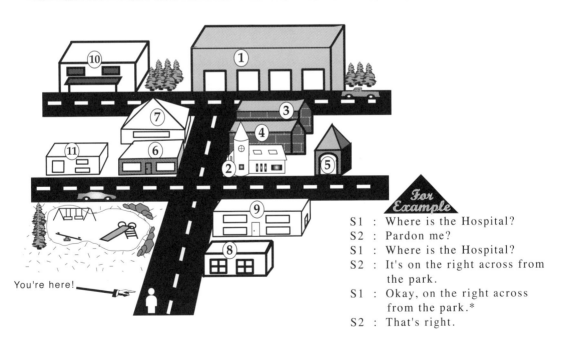

For Example

S1 : Where is the Hospital?
S2 : Pardon me?
S1 : Where is the Hospital?
S2 : It's on the right across from the park.
S1 : Okay, on the right across from the park.*
S2 : That's right.

Now, practice asking & giving the directions with your partner.

— 47 —

8

Speaker 1 page — Speaker 2 go to page # 102

For Example

Start at the fountian
Speaker 1 : Excuse me, how can I get to City Hall from here?

Speaker 2 : City Hall, Let me think. Go straight on First Avenue for two blocks and turn right. It's on the left across from the Used Clothes Shop.

Speaker 1 : Okay, so I go straight for two blocks and turn right. Is it on the left?

Speaker 2 : Yes, that's right.

Both Speakers have these places on their map.

> Fountain
> High Street Shopping Mall
> Museum of Natural History
> Pet Shop
> Police Box
> Roxy Dance Club
> Waldo's Books
> First National Bank
> Used Clothes Shop
> Holy Cross Church
> Bill's Bicycle Shop
> Apple Store
> Starbucks
> Yacht Club
> Driving Range
> Giant Pineapple

Grammar Hint

Usually "the" is not used for a specific name of a place but used for most others.

✗ The Kevin's Irish Pub
○ The Irish Pub
○ The Gas Station

2nd STEP — Places around town

Start from the fountain, ask Speaker 1 where these places are around town.

City Hall
Burger King
Public Library
Jewish Deli
Barber Shop
Church Street School
Liquor Store
Tower Records
Fruit Stand
Golden Diner
Grand Royal Hotel
Airport
Bus Station
Ross *(clothing store)*
Super View Movie Theater
Auto Shop
Tennis Club
Dental Clinic
University of Commerce

— 48 —

Which way is up?

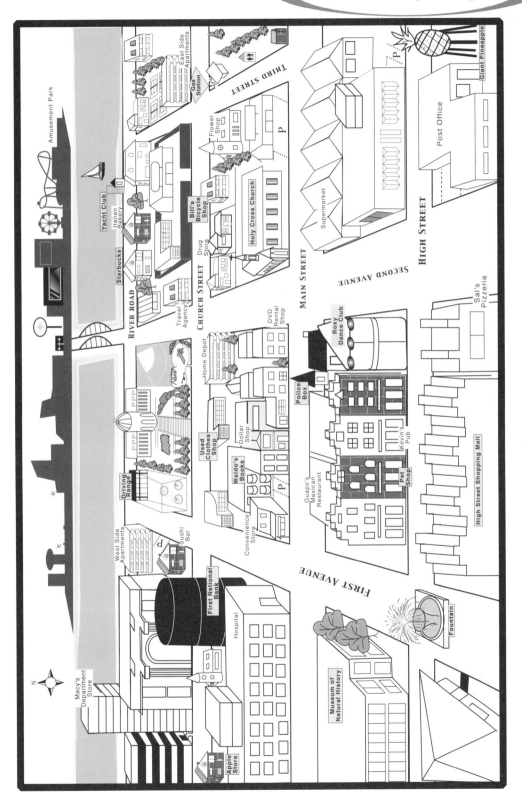

8

Draw a map from your house to the train station or bus stop.

3rd STEP

Which way is up?

Now, listen to your partner tell you how to get to his house.
Take notes and draw a simple map to the house.
Ask : How can I get to your house?
or Could you tell me the way to your house?

Some Useful words : a half block, one block, two blocks,
cross the train tracks, cross the bridge, along the river, at

8

Places Around Town Crossword Puzzle

Need to Know.

Home Center	City Hall	Restaurant	Dental Clinic
Gas Station	Station	Video Shop	Deli
Police Station	Zoo	Liquor Store	Drug Store
Flower Shop	Bank	Department Store	Museum
Cafe	Mall	Parking Lot	Barber Shop
Supermarket	Library	Book Store	Pet Shop
Butcher Shop	Hospital	Movie Theater	Fast Food
Post Office	Stadium	Convenience Store	Bus Stop

— 52 —

Which way is up?

ACROSS ✳——————→

2. I'm hungry. Do you know a good _____ around here?
4. Speaker 1 : Pardon me, Is there a library around here?
   Speaker 2 : No, but the _____ (two words) across the street sells all kinds of reading materials.
6. I need some money, can we stop at the _____?
10. The _____ _____ (two words) on the corner sells international beer, wine and whiskey.
11. There is a modern art exhibition at the _____ . Would you like to go and check it out?
12. In Japan, at the _____ (two words), not only can you buy stamps and send packages, but you can pay bills and get cash.
14. The place to go if you need help or to report a crime.
    _____ _____ (two words)
15. The place to go to learn about where you live and also pay our taxes. _____ (two words)
16. The _____ is a great place to study and learn, where you can borrow and read books.
17. We have no food. Let's go shopping at the _____.
18. Speaker 1 : Where is the _____ . (two words)
    Speaker 2 : Turn left and it's in front of the gas station. You will see people waiting in line for the next one.

✳ DOWN

1. We are out of milk, could you go to the _____? It's open 24 hours a day. (two words)
3. A place where you can watch live events. For example : sports or concerts.
5. From Grand Central _____ you can get a train to almost any major city in the U.S.
7. A place to buy things for your garden and house. (two words)
8. You need a doctor. Where is the closest _____?
9. Wow, look at the cute puppies and kittens in the window! This must be a _____. (two words)
13. Speaker 1 : I want to buy my mother a birthday present.
    Speaker 2 : You should go to the _____ (two words) and get her a bouquet of roses.

— 53 —

9

Practice the dialog with your partner

Jodi	:	Thanks for dinner, Mrs. Marco. It was really delicious.
Mrs. Marco	:	I'm glad you liked it.
Jodi	:	Can I help you clean up?
Mrs. Marco	:	Sure. I'll wash and you can put things away.
Jodi	:	Okay. Where does the <u>butter</u> go? (A1)
Mrs. Marco	:	It goes <u>in the refrigerator</u>. (B1)
Jodi	:	Where do the <u>napkins</u> go? (A2)
Mrs. Marco	:	They go <u>in the top drawer</u>. (B2)
Jodi	:	And where should I put this last piece of pie?
Mrs. Marco	:	Why don't you put it in your stomach?

Usage Hint

Singular Nouns Use : Does + it
Where does the soda go? It goes on the table.
Plural Nouns Use : Do + they/them
Where do the glasses go?
They go in the sink. / Put them in the sink.

Practice more by substituting the <u>underlined parts</u>.

	A1	B1	A2	B2
	frying pan	Under the sink	glasses	In the cabinet
	sugar bowl	On the counter	dishes	On the shelf
	pot	In the oven	knives	Under the sink
	dish towel	On the towel rack	salt and pepper shakers	On the table

Where does this go?

Cooperative Word Search

Things in the Living Room

Speaker 1 page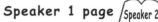

```
W T N A L P T I C N D L X R A Y T R D N
E L L A F P L S N M W T R C L Q E Z V K
P U X D L N E S C K J S I I E C C D I O
K N X G E C Z S G G H O S Y P J P J D E
S E R Q A B H E N Q W G E Y M L M X E R
E R U G O L Y C C F E J W S B L K G O E
D T N J N K V C A O E P U Y A U F E D T
M H Y B T W R D T Z V P Y V M C I H E S
M Y Y S I L J R C O M P U T E R K O C T
O A Z Q Y X P A E K C B Q N A W B O K I
E F H J Z I D C X U Z U B N Z G N Q O J
L O G P B K X K S P M S R X S Y N U N B
B S X N S A A I K V G K M T C L O S E T
A W T J I J M H O W T V I I A I R L O D
T K P A Y T S I O M Y B S Q P I N H G T
S D A B J H N I B V Y D A Y F J N C R P
M C L I P U A I X K P X C E L Y E S B C
A F S M V M A M A S C L T S J J N Q J I
Y B X Y P H K Z X P Q Z S F N H P Q L C
P Q R R T E F J O G P Y C P B B M H X O
```

Ask Speaker 2 for hints.

Things in the Living Room

① _____ ⑧ _____
② _____ ⑨ _____
③ _____ ⑩ _____
④ _____ ⑪ _____
⑤ _____ ⑫ _____
⑥ _____ ⑬ _____
⑦ _____ ⑭ _____

Circle the words when you find them.

For Example

Speaker 1 : Give me a hint.
Speaker 2 : Okay, It's big and square.
Speaker 1 : Is it a refrigerator?
Speaker 2 : No. Where do you put the glasses?
Speaker 1 : In the CABINET.
Speaker 2 : That's right!

GIVE HINTS ONLY!

Give Speaker 2 hints.

Things in the Kitchen

TABLE	STOVE
REFRIGERATOR	COUNTER
CABINET	TOASTER
CHAIR	SUGAR BOWL
MICROWAVE	GLASSES
SINK	DISHES
OVEN	SOAP
	TOWEL

Where does this go?

Draw a picture of a room in your house.

This is my _____

9

Listen and draw a picture of your partner's room.

Need to Know:

upper	in the
lower	middle
corner	next to
right side	in front of
left side	behind
	near upper

Speaker 1 : This is my room. First, put the bed the right corner.
Speaker 2 : Here?
Speaker 1 : Yes, then next to the bed put a small table.
Speaker 2 : About here?
Speaker 1 : No, on the other side.
   Next, there is a window on the back wall.
   To the left of the window, put a small TV.

This is my partner's _____

10 — All in the family

Wow, you really have a big family!

Practice the dialog with your partner

Sharon : Do you have a big family?

Meredith : No, I'm an only child.

Sharon : Oh, so you don't have any brothers or sisters?

Meredith : No, but I have lots of <u>cousins</u>. They're like brothers and sisters to me.

Sharon : There are five people in my family; My <u>mother, brother, sister, grandfather and me.</u>

Meredith : Is your <u>sister</u> older or younger than you?

Sharon : My <u>sister is older</u> than me.

Practice more by substituting the <u>underlined parts</u>.

Pets

Father, Mother, 2 Brothers

Aunts & Uncles

Father, 2 Sisters, Grandmother

Friends & Neighbors

Father, Mother, Sister, Uncle

Cousins

Mother, Brother, Sister, Grandfather

— 59 —

Study the Alien Family Tree. Use the words in the **"Need to know"** box to ask your partner questions about Hand Solo's family.

Need to Know.

brother	aunt
sister	uncle
mother	cousin
father	grandmother
husband	grandfather
wife	mother-in-law
son	father-in-law
daughter	sister-in-law
niece	brother-in-law
nephew	great grandmother
	great grandfather

For Example

Speaker 1 : Who is Paul Solo?
Speaker 2 : He is Hand's father.

Speaker 1 : What is his nephew's name?
Speaker 2 : His nephew's name is Philip.
   Who is Luke Skytalker's father?
Speaker 1 : That's easy! His father is Anikin Skytalker.

Alien Family Tree

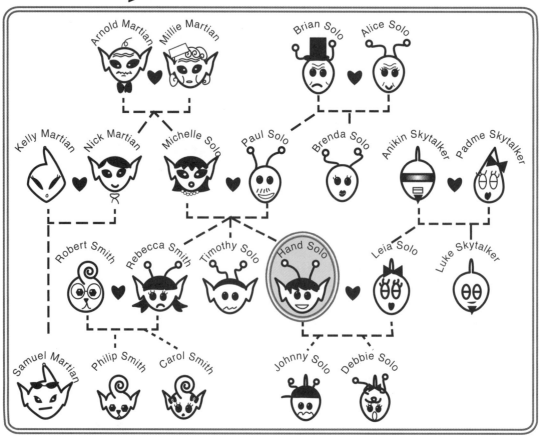

- 60 -

All in the family

Chuck

Listen and write the information about Chuck's family.

❋ _____

❋ _____

❋ _____

❋ _____

❋ _____

❋ _____

Draw a picture of your family.

Write your family information below, and tell your partner.

* There are ___ people in my family :

*

*

*

*

*

*

All in the family

Tell your partner about your family. Use the chart below to write your partner's information.

Do you have any brothers or sisters?
What is your sister's name?
What does your father do?
How old is your aunt?
When is your cousin's birthday?
Tell me something about your grandfather.

Usage Hint

Use these questions for clarification or for answers that you missed.

Wow! How many brothers & sisters do you have?

I have a really big family. There are 8 people in my family.

 Partner's Family

Relation	Name AGE	Occupation	Birthday	Other Information

 When finished check your answers by talking about your partners family.

Practice the dialog with your partner

Server	:	Hi there. Are you ready to order?
Customer	:	Yes. What's the soup of the day?
Server	:	Today's soup is <u>Clam Chowder</u> (1).
Customer	:	That sounds yummy! I'll have a cup, and the <u>sirloin steak</u> (2).
Server	:	Okay, how would you like your steak cooked?
Customer	:	<u>Medium rare</u> (3) please.
Server	:	That comes with a salad.
Customer	:	Oh, really? What kind of dressings do you have?
Server	:	We have Blue cheese, Ranch, French, and Italian.
Customer	:	Ummm. What do you recommend?
Server	:	The <u>Blue cheese</u> (4) is my favorite.
Customer	:	That'll* be fine.
Server	:	Would you care for anything to drink?
Customer	:	Just water, thanks.
Server	:	Okay, your food will be right out.

*that'll = that will

Practice more by substituting the <u>underlined parts</u>.

A
CONVERSATION

Server
(1) Vegetable
(4) French

Customer
(2) Filet mignon
(3) Rare

B
CONVERSATION

Server
(1) Chicken Noodle
(4) Ranch

Customer
(2) T-Bone
(3) Well done

Ready to order?

Describing Food

Color	:	Red, White
Size	:	Huge, small
Shape	:	Triangle, egg
Flavor	:	Strong, sour
Place of Origin	:	Peking, Africa
Kind	:	Vegetable, grain
Texture	:	Smooth, grainy
Cooking style	:	Raw, boiled

Questions for describing food.
What does it look like?

Color	:	What color is it?
Size	:	What is its size?
Shape	:	What is its shape?
Flavor	:	What does it taste like?
Place of Origin	:	Where is it from?
Kind	:	What kind is it?
Texture	:	What is its texture?
Cooking style	:	How is it cooked?

With your partner, brainstorm words to describe foods.
Only spend one minute for each category.

Color

Size

Shape

Flavor

Place of Origin

Kind

Texture

Cooking Style

Where are fried dumplings from?

I think they're originally from China.

2nd STEP — Make a list of foods and then describe them to your partner. Any kinds of foods are okay.
For Example : Apple, Caesar Salad, or Sukiyaki.

FOOD	DESCRIPTION (HINTS)
Bacon	meat/pork, salty, cooked in a frying pan

For Example

```
S1 : This meal needs many vegetables.
S2 : How is it cooked?
S1 : First the vegetables are chopped and then cooked.
S2 : Is it vegetable soup?
S1 : No, its not a soup. It's thicker than soup.
S2 : Where is it from? (place of origin)
S1 : Well, Japanese eat it all the time but I think its from India.
S2 : Is it curry?
S1 : Yes, that's right!
```

Listen to your partner describe food, and try and guess what it is.

DESCRIPTION (HINTS)	FOOD

3rd STEP

Circle the correct answer.

Ready to order?

QUICK FOOD QUIZ!

beef

cow

a jockey of beer

a mug of beer

french fries

fried potatoes

a cup of hot.

a cup of coffee.

ice cream soda

soda ice cream

salad

lettuce

ice cream cone

ice cream sundae

a whole pie

a piece of pie

half an apple

bunch of apple

roast turkey

bird meat

dog hot

hot dog

a bag of grapes

a bunch of grapes

3rd Step

Create your own menu, then give it to your partner to order.

EXAMPLE FOODS *(try and think of your own.)*

MAIN DISH	SALADS	BEVERAGES	SIDE DISHES
Leg of Lamb	Tuna	Soda (Coke, Pepsi)	Mashed Potatoes
Pork Chops	Fruit	Juices	Onion Rings
Lasagna	Pasta	Tea	Fried Onions
Spaghetti		Alcoholic drinks	Bread
Fried Oysters	**SOUPS**		**DESSERTS**
Steak	Minestrone		Vanilla Pudding
	Beef Barley		Strawberry Cheesecake
	Chicken Noodle		Chocolate Ice Cream

Example Questions for Customer

What kind of _____ do you have?
Do you have _____ ?
What do you recommend?

Usage Hint

Use the main dialog for help.

Ready to order?

Take turns being Server and Customer. Give a classmate your menu and use their book to write order. (change books)

Example Questions for server:

How would you like your

Hamburger?
(rare, medium, well done)

Coffee?
(with cream, sugar)

Tea?
(with lemon, milk, hot, cold)

What kind of

Salad Dressing?
(blue cheese, french)

Bread?
(white, wheat, rye)

Soda?
(orange, cola, lemon/lime)

Are you ready to order?

What size

Sorry we don't have _____ .

Will there be anything else?

Is that all?

Server Name : _____
Order Number : _____

Server Name : _____
Order Number : _____

Server Name : _____
Order Number : _____

For Example

Server : May I take your order?
Customer : Yes. Can I have the broiled shrimp platter.
Server : Broiled shrimp platter. That comes with fries and a vegtable.
Customer : Can I have a salad?
Server : Sure, anything else?
Customer : Yes, a large glass of milk and.....

Practice the dialog with your partner

Millie : Hi, long time no see.

Nick : Yeah, the last time we met was at Mike's <u>wedding</u> party.

Millie : Yes, the <u>lasagna</u> your wife made was to die for.

Nick : I'm glad you liked it. I'll be sure to let her know. Are those new <u>shoes</u>?

Millie : No, I've had them for a while.

Nick : No kidding. Where did you get them?

Millie : I got them at <u>Ross</u>. They were on sale.

Nick : Nice. And they really suit you.

Millie : How kind of you to say that.

Practice more by substituting the <u>underlined parts</u>.

	1	2	3
Nick	anniversary earrings	graduation gloves	birthday pants
Millie	salsa Target	apple pie Brooks Brothers	chilli The Gap

Why, Thank You!

1st STEP — Matching

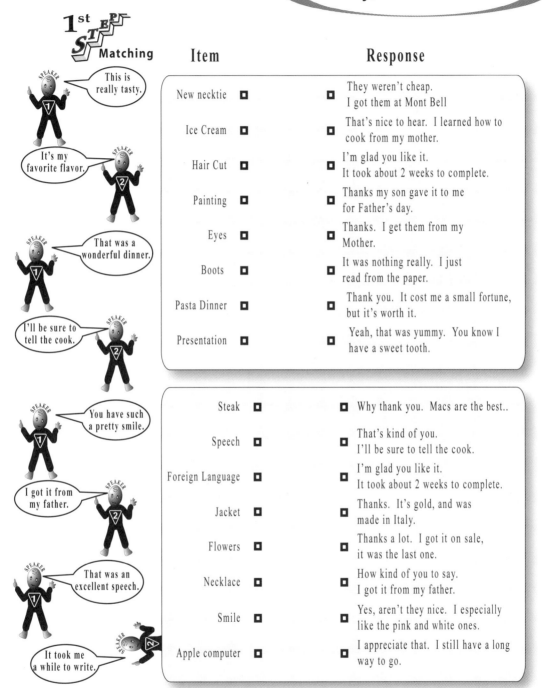

Speaker 1: This is really tasty.
Speaker 2: It's my favorite flavor.
Speaker 1: That was a wonderful dinner.
Speaker 2: I'll be sure to tell the cook.
Speaker 1: You have such a pretty smile.
Speaker 2: I got it from my father.
Speaker 1: That was an excellent speech.
Speaker 2: It took me a while to write.

Item	Response
New necktie	They weren't cheap. I got them at Mont Bell
Ice Cream	That's nice to hear. I learned how to cook from my mother.
Hair Cut	I'm glad you like it. It took about 2 weeks to complete.
Painting	Thanks my son gave it to me for Father's day.
Eyes	Thanks. I get them from my Mother.
Boots	It was nothing really. I just read from the paper.
Pasta Dinner	Thank you. It cost me a small fortune, but it's worth it.
Presentation	Yeah, that was yummy. You know I have a sweet tooth.

Item	Response
Steak	Why thank you. Macs are the best..
Speech	That's kind of you. I'll be sure to tell the cook.
Foreign Language	I'm glad you like it. It took about 2 weeks to complete.
Jacket	Thanks. It's gold, and was made in Italy.
Flowers	Thanks a lot. I got it on sale, it was the last one.
Necklace	How kind of you to say. I got it from my father.
Smile	Yes, aren't they nice. I especially like the pink and white ones.
Apple computer	I appreciate that. I still have a long way to go.

2nd STEP

Check your answers with your partner and practice.

12 FIND THE ERRORS

3rd STEP

Ask Speaker 2

Speaker 1 page

 Speaker 2 go to page # 73

For Example

A : In #1 I think ____ is a mistake.
B : That's right. (or) That's close (or) No, try again.
A : Is the correct answer ___ ?
B : That's right. (or) That's close (or) No, try again.
A : I give up.
B : It's ____.

That's a stinky looking hair cut.

Thanks, I got it at Speedy Cuts. They are slow and cheap.
(fast)

Find the mistake in the white box. | Tell your partner the correct answer.

Compliment | Response

① Your new hair shine looks super *(style)* Ms. Thomas. It really suits you. | How much of you to say so.

② I really like that old dress of *(new)* yours. Where did you sell it? *(buy)* | Oh, its not new. I stole it myself.

③ Your punch to the boss was *(presentation)* excellent. | Why thank you. It was everything.

④ That was a happy day you played. *(good game)* | Thanks I guess all the fireworks are finally paying off.

⑤ That was delicious. Was that a hint of death I tasted? | Thank you, and yes it should. *(is)*

⑥ Chef, that was the best tasting blueberry ham I have ever had. | Thank you sir I appreciate you kissing so. *(saying)*

⑦ That is a red drawing. | I appreciate that. If you like, you can eat it. *(have)*

⑧ Your cap has really improved. | I've been drinking hard at *(working)* my pronunciation.

Finished? Practice saying again with partner and memorize.

3rd STEP

FIND THE ERRORS
Ask Speaker 1

Speaker 2 page

Speaker 1 go to page # 72

Why, Thank You!

A : In #1 I think ____ is a mistake.
B : That's right. (or) That's close (or) No, try again.
A : Is the correct answer ___ ?
B : That's right. (or) That's close (or) No, try again.
A : I give up.
B : It's ____.

| That's a stinky looking hair cut. | Thanks, I got it at Speedy Cuts. They are slow and cheap. *(fast)* |

Find the mistake in the white box. | *Tell your partner the correct answer.*

	Compliment	Response
①	Your new hair shine looks super Ms. Thomas. It really suits you.	How much of you to say so. *(kind)*
②	I really like that old dress of yours. Where did you sell it?	Oh, its not new. I stole it myself. *(made)*
③	Your punch to the boss was excellent.	Why thank you. It was everything. *(nothing)*
④	That was a happy day you played.	Thanks I guess all the fireworks *(private lessons)* are finally paying off.
⑤	That was delicious. Was that a hint of death I tasted? *(garlic)*	Thank you, and yes it should.
⑥	Chef, that was the best tasting blueberry ham I have ever had. *(pie)*	Thank you sir I appreciate you kissing so.
⑦	That is a red drawing. *(beautiful)*	I appreciate that. If you like, you can eat it.
⑧	Your cap has really improved. *(English)*	I've been drinking hard at my pronunciation.

Finished? Practice saying again with partner and memorize.

- 73 -

12 — WALKABOUT

Why, Thank You!

Use It

Walk around the room and give compliments to your classmates.

A: Hi there. I really like your necklace (item).
(compliment)
B: Well thanks a lot, I like it too.
(response)
A: My name is Taro (name). May I ask your name?

B: Sure. I'm Hiroko (name)

ITEM : _____   COMPLIMENT : _____

RESPONSE : _____ WHO : _____

ITEM : _____   COMPLIMENT : _____

RESPONSE : _____ WHO : _____

ITEM : _____   COMPLIMENT : _____

RESPONSE : _____ WHO : _____

ITEM : _____   COMPLIMENT : _____

RESPONSE : _____ WHO : _____

ITEM : _____   COMPLIMENT : _____

RESPONSE : _____ WHO : _____

ITEM : _____   COMPLIMENT : _____

RESPONSE : _____ WHO : _____

13 Hit or Miss

How to play

1. Draw 7 ships anywhere on your battle grid.

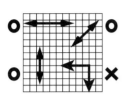

Your Fleet

Submarine

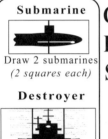

Draw 2 submarines
(2 squares each)

Destroyer

Draw 3 destroyers
(3 squares each)

Battleship

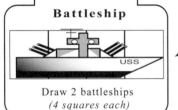

Draw 2 battleships
(4 squares each)

2. Take turns saying different places. Mark your partner's shots in the small battle grid.

Speaker 1 : 8pm **at the** library!
Speaker 2 : That's a miss!
              Noon at the pet shop.
Speaker 1 : That's a hit!

Your mission is to destroy all the enemy ships.

'TIME'

Your Sea-Battle Grid	am 9	10	11	12	1	2	3	pm 4	5	6	7	8
Zoo												
Drug Store												
Station												
Mall												
Pet Shop												
Disco												
Car Wash												
Stadium												
Restaurant												
School												
Library												
Internet Cafe												

P L A C E S

"The Library!"   "MISS!"   "HIT!"   "You sank my Battleship!"   "Hit and Sunk!"

Your partner's Sea-Battle Grid	am 9	10	11	12	1	2	3	pm 4	5	6	7	8
Zoo												
Drug Store												
Station												
Mall												
Pet Shop												
Disco												
Car Wash												
Stadium												
Restaurant												
School												
Library												
Internet Cafe												

BINGO!

How to play

1. Make small groups of 3-6 students.
2. One person is the "Speaker", the others are "players".
3. "Players" go to page 73-74 and choose a bingo game grid.
4. The "Speaker" makes sentences using the pictures on the Speaker page.
5. Players mark their grid when they hear the words that match the pictures.

For Example

Speaker : Okay, next. Tomorrow I will go "**Swimming**" with my "**cousin**". *(repeat a two times if needed)*

Speaker : Okay next. Last night I "**read a book**" and went to bed at "**midnight**". *(repeat a two times if needed)*

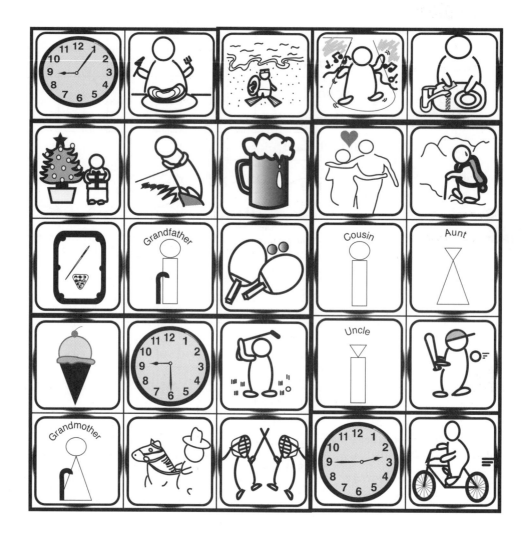

Practice makes Perfect

Speaker Page

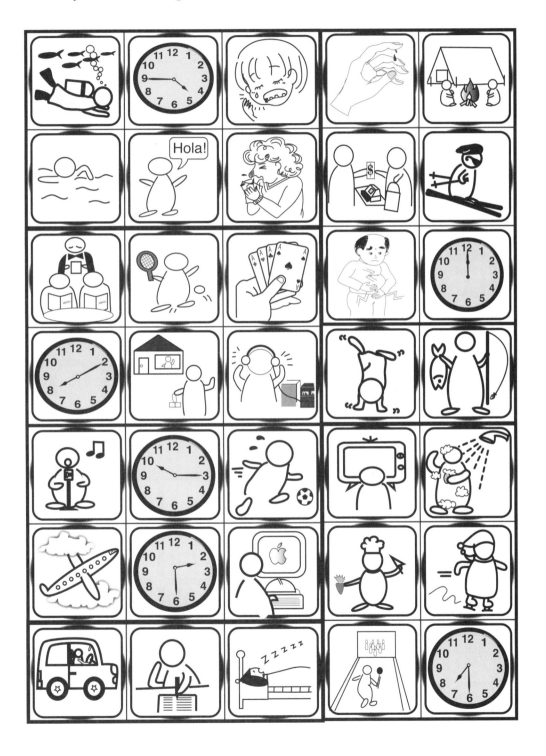

13

BINGO!

How to play
Choose a grid and listen to the Speaker.
Mark your grid when you hear the words.

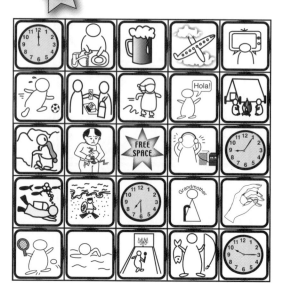

Practice makes Perfect

BINGO!

Choose a grid and listen to the Speaker.

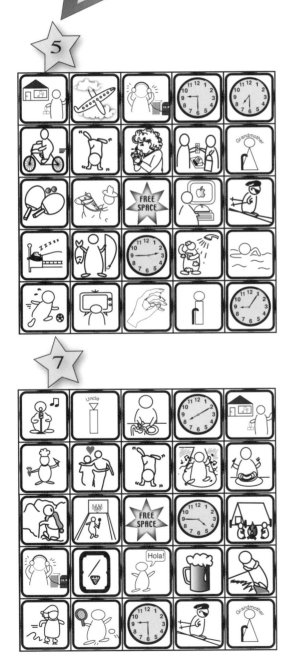

13

Where is Minnesota?

Ask student 2 about the states you are missing

Speaker 1 page

For Example

Speaker 1 : Where is Minnesota?
Speaker 2 : It's to the north. Just to the left of Wisconsin.

Practice makes Perfect

Usage Hint

Directions :
It's to the north.
It's north of Iowa.

Need to Know.
to the right
close to
next to
diagonal to
northeast
southwest

States that are circled, both speakers have. Answer Key on P. #100.

States you are missing

KANSAS	KS	ILLINOIS	IL	MICHIGAN	MI
ALASKA	AK	INDIANA	IN	MINNESOTA	MN
ARIZONA	AZ	IOWA	IA	MISSISSIPPI	MS
CONNECTICUT	CT	ALASKA	AK	NORTH CAROLINA	NC
DELAWARE	DE	LOUISIANA	LA	SOUTH DAKOTA	SD
FLORIDA	FL	MAINE	ME	VERMONT	VT
HAWAII	HI	MARYLAND	MD	WEST VIRGINIA	WV

SKIT

What is a skit?
A skit is a short, usually comic, dramatic performance.

Your grade :
You will be graded on your performance.
Your classmates will use this scorecard to check your performance.

Group Number / Student Name		Memorized	Team Work	Volume	Gestures Voice Inflection	Interesting	Total Score
Interviewer # 1	Mayu Nishioka	4	4	2	3	5	18/25
Interviewer # 2	Shinji Hayashi	1	4	4	1	3	13/25
Applicant # 1	Yoshi Urai	5	4	2	2	3	16/25
Applicant # 2							/25
Applicant # 3							/25
Applicant # 4							/25
						Total Group Score	/

EXAMPLE

You will be evaluated on 5 main points:

1. <u>Memorization</u>   : Did you memorized your lines? Did you speak smoothly, pausing at the correct times?

2. <u>Team Work</u>   : Did you work well with the other members? Did it sound natural and smooth?

3. <u>Volume/voice</u>   : Could everyone hear clearly what you were saying?

4. <u>Voice Inflection</u> : Did you change your tone, using inflection to express the meaning?

   <u>Gestures</u>   : Did you use body language and facial expressions?

5. <u>Interesting</u>   : Did you do something new, creative, funny, and surprising?

14

Listen and write which type of Voice inflection your hear.

Voice inflection is the way you change your voice to express a word or sentence.

Voice inflection is important because it gives your speech variation and change, helping the audience stay interested and understand you better.

There are 3 basic types of voice inflection :

< or >

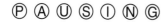

< or >

1. You paid too much for that jacket.

2. We are having a big sale.

3. The weather is going to be clear and sunny.

4. Did you do your homework?

5. Wow that was really interesting.

6. It costs 100 dollars.

7. That was the best sandwich I have ever had.

8. I have a good reason for being late.

Practice more by thinking of your more sentences and say them to your partner.

SKIT

Gestures and body language.

The way you move your hands and body help express what you want to say and make it easier for the listeners to understand.

Communicate the words below using gestures and body language.

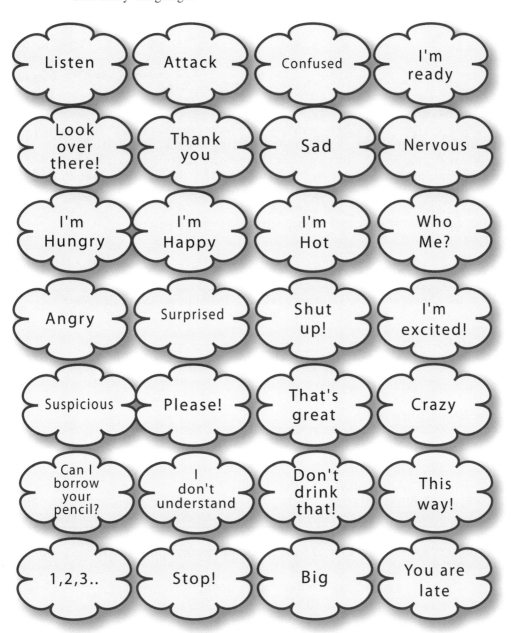

Listen	Attack	Confused	I'm ready
Look over there!	Thank you	Sad	Nervous
I'm Hungry	I'm Happy	I'm Hot	Who Me?
Angry	Surprised	Shut up!	I'm excited!
Suspicious	Please!	That's great	Crazy
Can I borrow your pencil?	I don't understand	Don't drink that!	This way!
1,2,3..	Stop!	Big	You are late

suspicious = あやしい

LAKE VIEW FREAK SHOW
Final Job Interviews.

Characters

Applicant 1	(A1)	
Applicant 2	(A2)	
Applicant 3	(A3)	
Applicant 4	(A4)	
Interviewer 1	(I1)	*Kind & friendly personality*
Interviewer 2	(I2)	*Snobby & arrogant personality*

Applicant advice

Congratulations you are very close to getting a great job, with the Lake View Freak Show. But you still have one more interview to pass. The most important part of the interview is the two minute speech and your special talent. You must speak for two minutes and then show your special skill or talent for the show.
In your speech you may talk about anything you like.
Some good topics are :

Self Introduction
Talk about yourself. What do you like? Your life, your part time, your hobbies, your studies, your personality. Talk about your childhood or your future. Why you want to join the show?

Your family
Tell them about your family. "There are four people in my family, my mother, my brother, my dog Spot and me."
Name, age, job, interesting points or hobbies.

House/home town
Where are you from? Where do you live? Do you like it? Why?
What interesting thing are there in your town or area?

Your special talent
Where/when did you learn it? Why is it special?
Make a story about your talent.

After your speech you must do a trick. This can be anything you like for example :

magic	sing
juggle	music instrument
sports	special talent
dance	impressions
card trick	crazy act

SKIT

LAKE VIEW FREAK SHOW Final Job Interviews.

I1 *(loud voice)* Good morning everyone, and thank you for coming to the final part of our interview.
As you know, the Lake View Freak Show is famous for its amazing acts and performances. We have been providing quality freak shows for over 20 years. I'm sure you can remember some of our big stars; the bearded lady, the goldfish eater, and don't forget the talking poodle, Gabby. This year we are looking for a new attraction.
Yes! One of you will become the new star of the Lake View Freak Show! *(Excited, looking at applicants)*

I2 *(Serious)* We are looking for a bright new star, someone who can do something funny and interesting. It has been very difficult to select the right person. This group has been chosen from over 1,000 others! You are the best of that group. Congratulations! You have made it to the last part of the interview.

I1 In this part of the interview, you must show us what freaky act you can do.
(Slow & serious, looking at applicants) First, we will ask some important questions and then you can, demonstrate, I mean show us, what special talents you have. The one with the most original and interesting talent will become the next Star of the Lake View Freak Show! Good luck!

I2 Now we are ready to start the interview. Applicant number one? *(Applicant #1 raise your hand)* Please sit here *(Point to the chair)* and would the other applicants please wait.

A1 Thank you. *(Sitting down)*

I1 Please tell us your name.

A1 My name is _____ .*(Your name)*

I1 Mr. / Ms. _____ *(Repeat name)*?

A1 Yes, that's right.

I1 Ok Mr. / Ms. _____ *(Repeat name)*, we are going to ask you some questions, please answer to the best of your knowledge.

A1 Okay!

I2 What is your shoe size? *(Say very quickly)*

A1 Excuse me? *(Look confused)*

– 85 –

I2   Shoe size. *(Lift up foot, point to shoe)* Tell us, what size shoes do you wear. *(A little angry)*

A1   Oh, yes, uh, _____ *(shoe size number)*, I wear a size _____ *(Shoe size number)*.

I2   *(Interviewer 1 & 2 act like writing notes)* Okay. What hurts on your body? Have you had a pain or ache lately?

A1   Hummm. Yes. *(Answer)*

I2   What happened?

A1   *(Answer, explain what happen to you)*

I2   Now please tell us what you can do and demonstrate your special talent.

A1   Thank you. I have many talents.
(Talk for at least 2 minutes and then do something funny)

I1   Wow, that was really interesting. Where did you learn how to do that?

A1   *(answer)*

I1   Next! Have a seat. *(Point to the chair)*

A2   Sure. *(Sitting down)*

I1   How are you today?

A2   Good, but a little nervous. *(Nervous gesture)*

I1   Oh, don't be nervous, just relax. Give me your name.

A2   *(Last name). (First name-last name)*

I1   Could you repeat that?

A2   *(Say again very slowly and loud.)*

I1   Uh, Do you know where the rest room is?

A2   *(Tell the way to the toilet)* *(check chapter 8, giving directions)*

LAKE VIEW FREAK SHOW

SKIT

Final Job Interviews.

I1   Thanks *(get up and walk out of room.)*

I2   All right, what is your shoe size?

A2   *(Say shoe size)*

I2   Do you have a pet?

A2   Yes, I have a _____. His name is _____*(pet's name)*.

I2   When is _____ 's *(pet's name)* birthday?

A2   _____'s birthday? *(Surprised)*

I2   Yeah, you know! *(Sing happy birthday for about 10 seconds)*

A2   *(answer)*

I2   What is your favorite color?

A2   *(answer)*

I2   Oh really. So is mine! *(Look suspicious & pause)* WHY?!

A2   *(answer)*

      (Interviewer 1 comes back and sits down.)

I2   Now please tell us what you can do and demonstrate your special talent.

A2   Sure, I'd be glad to. I can do many things....
      (Talk for 2 minutes and do something funny)
      (Interviewer 1 & 2 act like writing notes)

I2   Okay, are you finished?

A2 . That's all folks!

I2   *(Snobby & arrogant)* Okay, great, thank you that was really amazing.

      Thank you for your time we'll be in touch. (Point away)

A2   Thank you for your time.

I2   All right. Who's next! *(Loud voice)* Come in and sit down.

A3   Good day! *(come in and sit down)*

– 87 –

14 LAKE VIEW FREAK SHOW Final Job Interviews.

I2   State your name.

A3   My name is _____, and I'm from _____.

I2   Could you spell that?

A3   *(Start to spell the place where you are from)*

I2   *(Tired & angry,interrupt A3)* No-no-no!
Spell YOUR NAME! *(Slowly)*

A3   Oh yeah, sorry. *(Spell your last name)*
(Interviewers 1 & 2 look busy writing notes)

I1   Where do you live?

A3   *(Answer)*

I1   What part?

A3   *(Answer)*

I1   Where is that?

A3   *(Explain)*

I1   *(Look busy writing)* .... Okay, next. When do you usually take a shower?

A3   When do I take a shower? *(Look confused)*

I1   Yes. Exact time please. *(Smile)*

A3   uh...*(Answer)*

I1   Now please tell us what you can do and demonstrate your special talent.

A3   Sure, I'd be glad too. I can do many things....
(Talk for 2 minutes and do something funny)
(Interviewer 1 & 2 act like writing notes)

I2   Wonderful! Great! Fantastic! *(Look bored)*
Thank you, and remember, don't call us WE'LL call you. (Point away)

– 88 –

SKIT

A3   Have a nice day.

I1   Ok great, I guess that's everyone. *(Smile & get ready to finish)*

A4   *(Comes rushing in from outside)* Oh my god! Am I late?
What time is it?

I2   **(Very angry**) *(Say time)* The Lake View Freak Show interviews are
over! Unless you have a REALLY good excuse, I'm sorry.........

A4   (Interrupting) Oh no! I mean YES! I have a good reason for being
late. Please listen. *(explain why you were late)*

     (Interviewer 2 & 1 whispering to each other)

I2   Okay. You can have an interview, (Freak #4 very happy),

     but we have to hurry.

A4   Yes of course! *(Sitting down quickly and getting ready)*

I2   What's your name?

A4   *(answer)*

I2   Okay Mr. / Ms. _____ . Recite the months of the year.

A4   January.....*(say all)*

I2   Again, this time, backward. Start with December. *(Smiling)*

A4   *(Look shocked)(Answer)*

I1   Okay. Next. You are at a restaurant. What do you order?

A4   *(look confused)* I'm sorry, I don't get it.

I1   Alright, imagine I'm the waiter and you are the customer.
You can have anything you want, Okay? Are you ready to order?
(act like you are a waiter)

A4   Oh, I see! Yes I'm ready to order. I'll have *(say 3 or 4 things)*

_____

14 LAKE VIEW FREAK SHOW

SKIT
Final Job Interviews.

I2   Anything else?

A4   Yes, *(say more things)* _____ please.

I2   Humm, interesting. *(taking notes)* Now please tell us what you can do and demonstrate your special talent.

A4   Sure, I'd be glad too. I can do many things....
(Talk for 2 minutes and do something funny)

(Interviewer 1 & 2 act like writing notes)

I2   Wow! You really are a FREAK! Please wait over there for the results.

(Interviewer 2 & interviewer 1 whispering to each other)

I1   Thank you everyone for coming to the Lake View Freak Show final interview. We have reached our decision. It was really hard to choose. Everyone was so talented.

I2   So we have decided to hire all of you. *(Excited)* You will all become stars at the Lake View Freak Show! Congratulations!
(All applicants stand up and clap your hands.)

THE END

- 90 -

Interview Project

Interview with a foreigner

In this project you must interview a person from another country.

1. Make Questions.

Think of 10 questions to ask.

Your base questions may be as follows
What is your name?
Where do you live?
Where are you from?
May I ask your age?
Make your own questions…!

2. Prepare Equipment.

Record the interview or take photos.

You can use any kind of recording. Tape recorder, video recorder or, take pictures with a camera.

3. Analyze and Present Data.

Make a presentation to the class. The presentation should include a chart or poster to show your information. Everyone in the group must participate and it must be at least 6 minutes long.

Interview Check List ✓

- ☐ Our topic is : _____
- ☐ We have made _____ questions to ask.
- ☐ We will use a _____
  (equipment)
- ☐ We will interview _____
- ☐ The Date of our interview is : _____

- ☐ We will make our presentation on *(date)* : _____

Speaker 2 page

Ask your partner the time.

a   b   c   d

_____   _____   _____   _____

e   f   g   h

_____   _____   _____   _____

Usage Hint
Different Ways to ask the time.
What time is it?
Do you have the time?
Could you please tell me the time?
Do you know what time it is?
Can you tell me the time?

Speaker 2 Tell your partner the time.

1   2   3   4

5   6   7   8

What time does it start?

2nd STEP

Fill in the blanks by asking your partner.

Speaker 2 page

Speaker 1 go to page # 11

How to Ask
What's on (DAY) at / from (TIME) on (channel #)?
What's on (at/from) (TIME) on (channel #)?

Example:
What's on Friday from 9:30 on Channel 12?

How to Answer
(Program name) (is / are) on (at/from) (TIME) on (channel #)?

Example:
A documentary is on from 9 o'clock on channel 12.
<or>
Star Trek is on at 5 on channel 6.

	TIME	CHANNEL 3	CHANNEL 6	CHANNEL 10	CHANNEL 12
F R I D A Y	4:00 p.m.	Tom & Jerry		Vimbledon Tennis Championship	The Green Thumb
	4:30 p.m.	Peanuts			
	5:00 p.m.	Ultra Woman			
	5:30 p.m.				
	6:00 p.m.	Local News			
	6:30 p.m.		North Park	Game Show	
	7:00 p.m.		Variety Show	World News	
	7:30 p.m.				
	8:00 p.m.	Project B		"Yoshi My Love" *Romance Drama*	Goma Street
	8:30 p.m.				
	9:00 p.m.	"I Know You Didn't Do Your Homework!" *(Horror Movie)*		NEWS 21	
	9:30 p.m.				
	10:00 p.m.				
	10:30 p.m.				
	TIME	CHANNEL 3	CHANNEL 6	CHANNEL 10	CHANNEL 12
S A T U R D A Y	4:00 p.m.	G-Force	Samurai Drama	Gossip Show	*(write your answer)**
	4:30 p.m.	Black Jack			
	5:00 p.m.		Star Trek	The Oprah Winfrey Show	
	5:30 p.m.				
	6:00 p.m.	TV Shopping			
	6:30 p.m.		Funny Home Videos		
	7:00 p.m.		CSI :Tokyo		Two-Way Street *(Learn English)*
	7:30 p.m.				
	8:00 p.m.		"Madame Butterfingers"		
	8:30 p.m.				
	9:00 p.m.		*(Musical Special)*		"Under the Deep Blue Sea." *(Documentary)*
	9:30 p.m.				
	10:00 p.m.		London Sneakers		
	10:30 p.m.				

**Write your favorite TV show.*

2nd STEP Practice
Pair work with Speaker 1
Circle the correct answer

Chris

Janan

Andrew

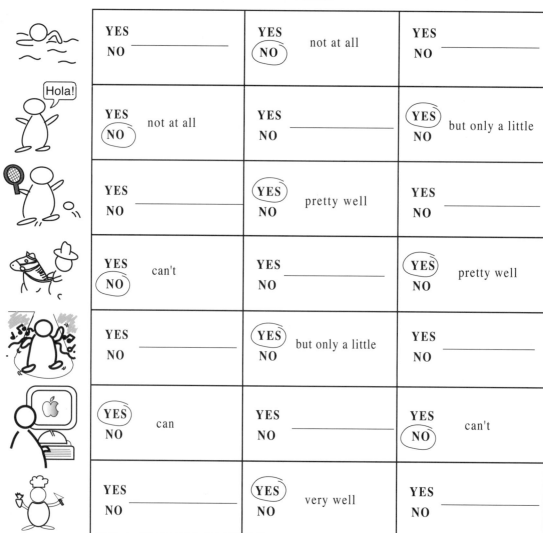

Do you know how to...?

S1 : Can Chris speak Spanish?
S2 : Nah, not at all. Can he swim?
S1 : Yes, he can.
<OR>
S2 : Can Emily dance?
S1 : Yeah, (she can) pretty well. Can she ride a horse?
S2 : Nah, not at all.

Speaker 2 page

	Emily	Rosebud	Jamie & Kim
	(YES) but not very well NO	YES _____ NO	(YES) they can NO
	YES _____ NO	YES (NO) cant	YES _____ NO
	(YES) she can NO	YES _____ NO	(YES) pretty well NO
	YES _____ NO	YES (NO) not at all	YES _____ NO
	(YES) pretty well NO	YES _____ NO	YES not at all (NO)
	YES _____ NO	YES not very well (NO)	YES _____ NO
	YES _____ NO	(YES) she can NO	YES _____ NO

3

1st STEP — PAST EVENTS & DATES   Speaker 2 page   Speaker 1 go to page # 15

Tell Speaker 2 the answers.

Answer

The start of the railways in Japan	6/1/1949
The World Trade Center bombing	9/11/2001
The US / Japan San Francisco Peace Treaty	4/28/1952
Miyazaki awarded Picture of the Year for Princess Mononoke	2/18/1998
The Atomic bomb dropped on Hiroshima	8/6/1945
The Showa era changed to The Heisei era	1/7/1989
The end of World War Two for Japan	8/15/1945
America's first independence day	7/4/1776
The end of US occupation in Okinawa	5/15/1972
The first moonwalk	7/20/1969

Ask Speaker 2, & write the answers.

 For Example

S1 : When was _____ ? *(event)*
S2 : It was _____. *(date)*

S1 : Tell me what happened on _____. *(date)*
(or) Do you know what happened on _____? *(date)*
S2 : _____ *(event)*

EVENT	DATE
Princess Diana's fatal car accident…………………	
The first Japanese woman in space………………	
President F.D. Roosevelt's "Four Freedoms" speech.	
The Japanese attack on Pearl Harbor……………	
Adolf Hitler named Chancellor of Germany…….	
	3/28/1869
	6/18/2000
	11/16/1963
	1/17/1995
	9/15/2003

Practice makes Perfect

ANSWERS for Correct It Sentence List

(BOARD GAME page #40-43)

- 1. It's a quarter past 11.
- 2. I can play baseball well.
- 3. Let's go downtown.
- 4. The pen is in my pocket.
- 5. The glass is on the table.
- 6. It's twelve thirty.
- 7. What are your hobbies?
- 8. What is your name?
- 9. How old are you?
- 10. Can you ski?
- 11. Did you go to school today?
- 12. What are your hobbies?
- 13. I have an apple.
- 14. I'm from Japan
- 15. Yes I can. / No I can't.
- 16. Do you know today's date?
- 17. Today is February second.
- 18. Nice to met you.
- 19. Can you *speak* English?
- 20. I was born *in* Osaka.
- 21. Do you *do / practice* Aikido?
- 22. Are you married?
- 23. Can she swim.
- 24. Yesterday I *watched* TV.
- 25. My birthday is October thirty-first.
- 26. Excuse me, do you have the time?
- 27. It's a police officer's job to stop crime.
- 28. A waitress works at a restaurant.
- 29. A mechanic can repair cars.
- 30. Never or always
- 31. He hardly ever misses class.
- 32. Excuse me, where is the toilet?
- 33. Excuse me, do you have the time?
- 34. What do you do?
- 35. I usually *eat* breakfast....
- 36. *We* live in a high-rise.....

6

3rd STEP

Ask Speaker 1

- Age & Occupation — How old is he/she? What does he/she do?
- What's Wrong? — What's wrong?
- What to do? — What should he/she do?
- What not to do? — What shouldn't he/she do?

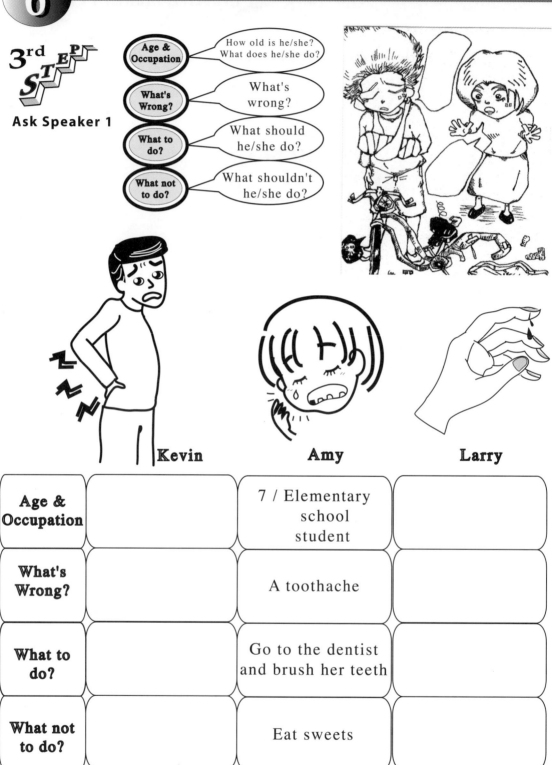

Kevin   Amy   Larry

	Kevin	Amy	Larry
Age & Occupation		7 / Elementary school student	
What's Wrong?		A toothache	
What to do?		Go to the dentist and brush her teeth	
What not to do?		Eat sweets	

Ouch! That hurts!

Speaker 1 : How old's Pete?
Speaker 2 : He's <u>17</u> years old.
Speaker 1 : What does he do?
Speaker 2 : He is <u>a mechanic</u>.
Speaker 1 : What's wrong?
Speaker 2 : He's <u>got a headache</u>.
Speaker 1 : What should he do?
Speaker 2 : He should <u>take two aspirin and get a massage</u>.
Speaker 1 : What shouldn't he do?
Speaker 2 : He shouldn't <u>listen to loud music or play video games</u>.

Speaker 2 page — Speaker 1 go to page # 38-39

Usage Hint

△ = She / her

▯ = He / his

Evan

Jiro

Angela

28 / Ski Instructor		21 / University student
The Flu*		A Fever
Take vitamins and go to bed early		Drink tea and stay warm
Take a bath		Go Outside

"the flu" is short for "influenza.

9

Cooperative Word Search

Things in the Kitchen

Speaker 2 page

Speaker 1 go to page # 56

```
G G L A S S E S G V M U C W X F T I J M
N N B N Y O E N D F A S C C Y O C G C Y
E U E Y H U F T M D E T Q X M Y Y R G Q
Q Q N Y U D O L P S N X N D I S K O D N
C Q F M O S O A P Q T Z R F C E A C D E
H L A K Y U R Q P F P Q O L R P L M W I
A G C X X E L Q G W A N T T O G C B O V
I S A M F W X L D K X Y A X W R L Z A M
R U C U I E K X P K X D R T A Q D L C T
R G W H J V C Z L R S Z E Y V S Y S P E
E A N I B F V Z V P E A G Y E G C J T C
T R H L W Q Y Y Y P K S I Q Z V E E U I
S B X U R R E T N U O C R R N B N S F X
A O L Z X S E W P O E S F R J I T Z J V
O W E S I O G K E B E Y E Y B O S I N K
T L W Y T R W M O H C I R A V E I T H I
M Q O S T Z P Z S H Q P C E V S A U A Q
B X T Q Q Y L I T R N K N U C P I H N X
M W H U V P D X Z K Y F C L A W R N M M
D P F Q W F R Y Z X G U Z E J L F D J V
```

Ask Speaker 1 for hints.

Things in the Kitchen

① _____ ⑧ _____
② _____ ⑨ _____
③ _____ ⑩ _____
④ _____ ⑪ _____
⑤ _____ ⑫ _____
⑥ _____ ⑬ _____
⑦ _____ ⑭ _____
　　　　　⑮ _____

Circle the words when you find them.

For Example

Speaker 1 : Give me a hint.
Speaker 2 : Okay, It's big and square.
Speaker 1 : Is it a refrigerator?
Speaker 2 : No. Where do you put the glasses?
Speaker 1 : In the CABINET.
Speaker 2 : That's right!

Give Speaker 1 hints.

Things in the Living Room

SOFA　　　　CLOSET
BOOKCASE　　CURTAINS
TABLE　　　　PLANT
DESK　　　　PAINTING
COMPUTER　　VIDEO DECK
RUG　　　　CD RACK
STEREO　　　BOOKS

- 100 -

Practice makes Perfect

Where is Minnesota?
List of all states abbreviations

ALABAMA	AL	KENTUCKY	KY	OKLAHOMA	OK
ALASKA	AK	LOUISIANA	LA	OREGON	OR
ARIZONA	AZ	MAINE	ME	PENNSYLVANIA	PA
ARKANSAS	AR	MASSACHUSETTS	MA	RHODE ISLAND	RI
CALIFORNIA	CA	MICHIGAN	MI	SOUTH CAROLINA	SC
COLORADO	CO	MINNESOTA	MN	SOUTH DAKOTA	SD
CONNECTICUT	CT	MISSISSIPPI	MS	TENNESSEE	TN
DELAWARE	DE	MISSOURI	MO	TEXAS	TX
FLORIDA	FL	MONTANA	MT	UTAH	UT
GEORGIA	GA	NEBRASKA	NE	VERMONT	VT
HAWAII	HI	NEVADA	NV	VIRGINIA	VA
IDAHO	ID	NEW HAMPSHIRE	NH	WASHINGTON	WA
ILLINOIS	IL	NEW JERSEY	NJ	WEST VIRGINIA	WV
INDIANA	IN	NEW MEXICO	NM	WISCONSIN	WI
IOWA	IA	NEW YORK	NY	WYOMING	WY
KANSAS	KS	NORTH CAROLINA	NC	ALABAMA	AL
		NORTH DAKOTA	ND	ALASKA	AK
		OHIO	OH	ARIZONA	AZ

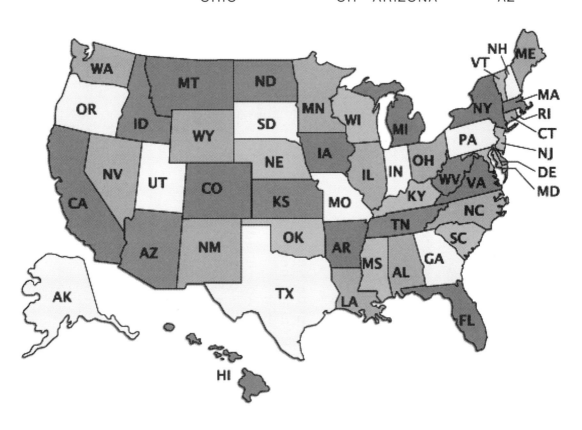

— 101 —

8

2nd STEP Places around town

Start from the fountain, ask Speaker 1 where these places are around town.

Flower Shop
Kevin's Pub
Home Depot
Hospital
Convenience Store
DVD Rental Shop
Sal's Pizzeria
East Side Apartments
West Side Apartments
Amusement Park
Supermarket
Guapo's Mexican Restaurant
Dollar Shop
Italian Bakery
Sushi Bar
Travel Agency
Macy's Department Store
Post Office

Speaker 2 page

Speaker 1 go to page # 48-9

For Example

Start at the fountian
Speaker 1 : Excuse me, how can I get to City Hall from here?

Speaker 2 : City Hall, Let me think. Go straight on First Avenue for two blocks and turn right. It's on the left across from the Used Clothes Shop.

Speaker 1 : Okay, so I go straight for two blocks and turn right. Is it on the left?

Speaker 2 : Yes, that's right.

Both Speakers have these places on their map.

Fountain
High Street Shopping Mall
Museum of Natural History
Pet Shop
Police Box
Roxy Dance Club
Waldo's Books
First National Bank
Used Clothes Shop
Holy Cross Church
Bill's Bike Shop
Apple Store
Starbucks
Yacht Club
Driving Range
Giant Pineapple

Grammar Hint
Usually "the" is not used for a specific name of a place but used for most others.

✗ The Kevin's Irish Pub
○ The Irish Pub
○ The Home Depot

— 102 —

Which way is up?

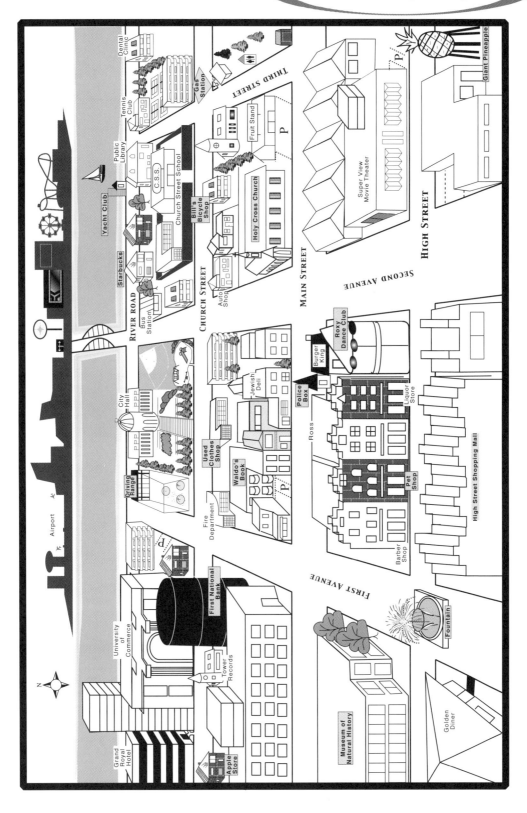

13 Where is Minnesota?

Practice makes Perfect

Ask student 1 about the states you are missing

Speaker 1 : Where is Minnesota?
Speaker 2 : It's to the north. Just to the left of Wisconsin.

Speaker 2 page

Speaker 1 go to page # 80

Usage Hint
Directions :
It's to the north.
It's north of Iowa.

Need to Know.
to the right
close to
next to
diagonal to
northeast
southwest

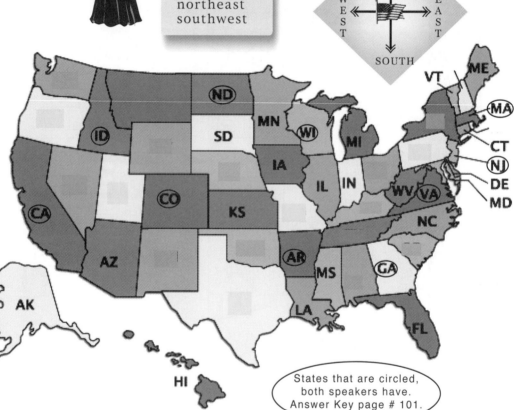

States that are circled, both speakers have. Answer Key page # 101.

States you are missing

ALABAMA	AL	NEW MEXICO	NM	SOUTH CAROLINA	SC
MISSOURI	MO	NEW YORK	NY	TENNESSEE	TN
KENTUCKY	KY	OHIO	OH	TEXAS	TX
MONTANA	MT	OKLAHOMA	OK	UTAH	UT
NEBRASKA	NE	OREGON	OR	WASHINGTON	WA
NEVADA	NV	PENNSYLVANIA	PA	WYOMING	WY
NEW HAMPSHIRE	NH	RHODE ISLAND	RI	ALABAMA	AL

■著者紹介

Michael Greisamer（マイケル グリーサマー）

最終学歴：University of Anaheim, California, USA
学　　位：Doctor of Education in TESOL（2017）
現　　在：神戸学院大学人文学部講師

TWO-WAY STREET

2011 年 4 月 11 日　初　版第 1 刷発行
2016 年 4 月 15 日　第 2 版第 1 刷発行

■著　　者──マイケル グリーサマー
■発 行 者──佐藤　守
■発 行 所──株式会社**大学教育出版**
　　　　　　　〒 700-0953　岡山市南区西市 855-4
　　　　　　　電話 (086) 244-1268 (代)　FAX (086) 246-0294
■印刷製本──サンコー印刷㈱

© Michael Greisamer 2016, Printed in Japan
検印省略　　落丁・乱丁本はお取り替えいたします。
本書のコピー・スキャン・デジタル化等の無断複製は著作権法上での例
外を除き禁じられています。本書を代行業者等の第三者に依頼してス
キャンやデジタル化することは、たとえ個人や家庭内での利用でも著作
権法違反です。

ISBN978-4-86429-369-3